Stocks and Options for Teens

Empowering Today's Youth with Financial Literacy and Investing Strategies

K. Thomas

medical or professional advice. The content within this book has been derived from various sources.

Please consult a licensed professional before attempting any techniques outlined in this book. By reading this document, the reader agrees that under no circumstances is the author responsible for any losses, direct or indirect, that are incurred as a result of the use of the information contained within this document, including, but not limited to, errors, omissions, or inaccuracies.

Table of Contents

Introduction

"Success is not final, failure is not fatal: It is the courage to continue that counts." - Winston Churchill

Securing Your Financial Future: Embrace the Power of Investing

Attention, teens! Have you ever wondered why some people seem to have a magical ability to turn their money into even more money? It's not magic—it's investing! Let us reveal the secrets of this incredible world and show you why it's crucial for your future.

Imagine having a magic money tree that grows bigger and bigger, providing you with financial security and freedom. That tree is investing! By setting aside a portion of your hard-earned money and allowing it to grow through investments, you're planting the seeds for an abundant future.

Investing teaches us the value of patience and discipline. Instead of spending every penny we earn, we choose to save and invest, letting our money work for us while we focus on other things. By investing, we create a pathway to financial independence and the ability to achieve our dreams.

Among the many investing options available,
stocks and **options** shine as the stars of this
financial galaxy. Why are they so popular? Because
they offer incredible opportunities for growth and
profits!

Stocks are like owning a tiny piece of a company. As
the company succeeds and profits increase, the
value of your stocks can skyrocket, turning your
small investment into a sizable fortune. By
investing in stocks, you become a part-owner of
these amazing enterprises, sharing in their
successes and reaping the rewards.

Options, on the other hand, are like possessing a
superpower in the investing world. They give you
the right to buy or sell stocks at a predetermined
price within a specific time frame. This flexibility
allows you to amplify your returns and protect
yourself from potential losses. Options empower
you with strategic choices in the ever-changing
stock market.

By engaging in stocks and options, you learn
invaluable life skills – critical thinking, risk
assessment, and the ability to make informed
decisions. These skills will serve you not only in the
financial realm but also in various aspects of life.

Investing is not just for adults; it's a stepping stone
to financial success at any age. So, teens, seize the

opportunity to learn about investing now! Explore the captivating world of stocks and options. Let your money grow and watch your dreams flourish!

Remember, investing is a lifelong journey. Start early, and you'll reap the benefits for years to come. Embrace the power of investing and set yourself on a path to a prosperous and fulfilling future!

While teens may have an interest in learning about stocks and investing, it's important to note that the legal and financial requirements for trading stocks typically restrict such activities to individuals who are at least 18 years old. However, teens can still take steps to gain knowledge and develop skills related to investing. Here are some suggestions:

Educate Yourself: Begin by learning about basic financial concepts, such as stocks, markets, investing, and risk. There are numerous online resources, books, and educational platforms that provide information specifically designed for younger audiences. Take advantage of these resources to build a solid foundation of knowledge.

Talk to Parents/Guardians: Discuss your interest in investing with your parents or guardians. They can provide guidance and support, and may even be willing to help you open a custodial account to invest in stocks until you come of legal age.

Practice Investing: Some investment websites or apps offer virtual or simulated trading platforms that allow you to practice investing with virtual money. These platforms can provide a safe and risk-free environment to learn and develop investment skills.

Follow the Market: Stay updated on financial news and current events that may impact the stock market. This can help you understand how various factors influence stock prices and investment decisions.

Consider Long-Term Investing: Focus on long-term investing rather than short-term trading. Preteens have a significant advantage through the power of **compounding** over time. Early investments made with a long-term perspective can potentially grow substantially by the time you reach adulthood.

Seek Guidance from Adults: Engage with adults who have an understanding of investing, such as family members, teachers, or mentors. They can offer advice and insights based on their own experiences.

Remember, it's crucial to build a strong financial foundation and understand the risks associated with investing. Developing good financial habits, such as budgeting, saving, and responsible spending, are essential skills to master before venturing into investing.

Benefits Of Financial Literacy

Acquiring financial literacy brings numerous benefits that can significantly impact an individual's life. Here are some key advantages:

> **Making Informed Decisions:** Financial literacy equips individuals with the knowledge and skills to make informed decisions regarding their finances. It enables them to understand concepts such as budgeting, saving, investing, and borrowing. With this knowledge, they can make smart choices about how to manage their money, weigh risks and rewards, and plan for the future.

> **Achieving Financial Independence:** Financial literacy empowers individuals to achieve financial independence. By understanding and applying principles of personal finance, such as budgeting, saving, and investing wisely, people can take control of their financial situation. They can

work towards financial goals, minimize debt, build emergency funds, and ultimately attain greater financial stability and freedom.

Becoming Responsible Citizens: Financial literacy cultivates responsible citizenship. When individuals have a good understanding of personal finance, they are less likely to rely on public assistance programs or fall into financial hardships that may require taxpayer-funded support. By managing their finances effectively, they contribute to the overall economic well-being of their community and society.

Building Wealth and Security: Financial literacy helps individuals work towards building wealth and creating financial security. By understanding concepts like investing, compounding interest, and **diversification**, individuals can make informed decisions to grow their wealth over time. They can also protect themselves against financial risks and develop long-term financial strategies for retirement or other long-term goals.

Minimizing Financial Stress: Financial literacy equips individuals with skills to manage and reduce financial stress. It provides them with tools to develop a budget, plan for unexpected expenses, and avoid unnecessary debt. By being financially literate, individuals gain a sense of control over their finances, leading to reduced stress and improved overall well-being.

Navigating Economic Challenges: Financial literacy helps individuals navigate economic challenges and fluctuations. It enables them to adapt to changes, make strategic financial decisions during uncertain times, and protect themselves from financial pitfalls. This resilience can serve individuals well in times of economic downturn or personal financial setbacks.

Overall, acquiring financial literacy enables individuals to make well-informed decisions, achieve financial independence, become responsible citizens, build wealth, minimize stress, and navigate economic challenges effectively. It is a valuable and empowering skill set that positively influences various aspects of life.

Knowledge Is Power

The power of knowledge is an incredible tool for everyone, including teens. Knowledge refers to the information, facts, and understanding that one gains through learning and exploration. Here are a few ways to explain the power of knowledge:

Empowerment: Knowledge empowers you to have control over your own life. When you have knowledge, you can make informed choices and decisions. For example, if you know about different hobbies or activities, you can choose one that genuinely interests you, making your free time more enjoyable.

Learning and Growth: Knowledge opens up opportunities for learning and personal growth. The more you learn, the more you can develop your skills and expand your horizons. This can lead to new and exciting experiences, friendships, and personal achievements.

Problem-Solving: Knowledge equips you with problem-solving skills. When you have knowledge on a particular subject, you can better understand problems and find solutions. It helps you think critically, explore different perspectives, and come up with creative ideas to overcome challenges.

Confidence: Knowledge gives you confidence in yourself and your abilities. The more you know about a topic or subject, the more confident you'll feel discussing or participating in conversations about it. Confidence can positively impact your self-esteem and help you navigate various aspects of life.

Independence: Knowledge helps you become independent and self-reliant. When you possess knowledge, you have the ability to explore and understand things on your own. You don't have to rely solely on others for information or solutions, which promotes autonomy and resourcefulness.

Success: Knowledge can lead to success in different areas of life. It helps you acquire skills, understand concepts, and make better choices. It can open doors to educational and career opportunities, as well as enrich your personal life. knowledge is something you will continue to gain throughout your life and that it is an essential tool for personal growth and success.

Chapter 1: Stock Market Basics

"The only limit to our realization of tomorrow will be our doubts of today." - Franklin D. Roosevelt

The **stock market** is a financial market where individuals and entities can buy and sell shares of publicly traded companies. It is a platform that facilitates the trading of stocks, which represent ownership in a company. The stock market is also referred to as the equity market or the share market.

In the stock market, companies sell shares of their ownership to raise capital, and individuals or institutional investors (such as mutual funds or pension funds) can purchase these shares as investments. The stock market provides a way for companies to raise funds and for investors to potentially earn profits by buying and selling stocks.

The stock market operates through exchanges, such as the **New York Stock Exchange (NYSE)** and **NASDAQ**. These exchanges provide a platform where buyers and sellers can place orders to trade stocks. The prices of stocks listed on the stock market are determined by supply and demand dynamics, influenced by factors such as company performance, economic conditions, investor sentiment, and news events.

The stock market plays a crucial role in the economy as it allows companies to raise capital for growth and expansion, and it provides individuals and institutional investors with opportunities to invest their savings and potentially earn returns. It is important to note that investing in the stock market carries risks, as stock prices can fluctuate and investor returns are not guaranteed.

Stock Market Purposes

Capital Formation: Companies can raise capital by issuing stocks or bonds to investors through an **initial public offering (IPO)** or subsequent offerings. This capital can then be utilized for business expansion, research and development, acquisitions, or debt repayment, fostering economic growth.

Liquidity: The stock market provides liquidity, enabling investors to buy or sell securities quickly and at a fair price. Liquidity ensures that investors can easily convert their investments into cash, which promotes financial flexibility and reduces risks associated with illiquid assets.

Price Discovery: The stock market helps establish the price of **securities** by facilitating the buying and selling activity. The forces of supply and demand interact in the market, influencing the prices of securities. This price discovery mechanism reflects the perceived value of securities based on various factors, such as company earnings, economic conditions, and market sentiment.

Investment Opportunities: The stock market offers individuals and institutional investors a wide range of investment opportunities. Investors can allocate their **capital** across various sectors, industries, and regions to diversify their **portfolios** and potentially earn returns through capital appreciation and dividends.

Risk Management: The stock market provides tools, such as **derivatives** (e.g., futures and options), that allow investors to hedge their investment risks. Derivatives enable investors to protect against price fluctuations, manage **volatility**, and reduce exposure to potential losses.

Transparency and Regulation: Stock exchanges operate under specific regulations to ensure fair and transparent trading practices. Regulatory bodies monitor the exchanges, listed companies, and participants to maintain market integrity, protect investors, and prevent fraudulent activities.

Overall, the stock market plays a crucial role in the functioning of the economy by facilitating capital formation, providing liquidity, and offering investment opportunities, while also contributing to price fluctuation and risk management.

The Essentials Of Stock Investing

Research and Analysis: Before investing in stocks, it is crucial to thoroughly research and analyze the companies you are interested in. This includes understanding their business model, financial health, competitive advantages, industry trends, and growth potential. Use varying forms of analysis to make informed investment decisions.

Diversification: Diversification is an essential strategy to mitigate risk. By investing in a diversified portfolio of stocks across different **sectors**, **industries**, and geographic locations, you can reduce the impact of any single stock's performance on your overall investment. This spreads risk and potentially improves returns.

Long-Term Perspective: Stock investing is typically a long-term endeavor. It is important to have a disciplined approach and a patient mindset. Short-term market fluctuations can be unpredictable, but historically, stocks have provided attractive returns over the long term. Avoid emotional decision-making and don't get swayed by short-term market sentiment.

Risk Management: Understand and manage your risk tolerance. Investing in stocks involves inherent risks, such as market volatility and the potential for loss. Assess your risk appetite and make investment decisions accordingly. Consider setting **stop-loss orders** or using techniques like **dollar-cost averaging** to manage risk.

Fundamental Analysis: Focus on the fundamental factors that drive a company's value, such as earnings growth, revenue growth and **profitability**. Use financial ratios and key indicators to evaluate a company's financial health and valuation. This will help you make more informed investment decisions.

Keep Yourself Informed: Stay updated with market and industry news and developments. Regularly review the performance of your portfolio and make adjustments if necessary. Being well-informed about your investments is key to making sound decisions.

Consider Professional Advice: If you are new to stock investing or lack the time or expertise to thoroughly analyze stocks, consider seeking professional advice from financial advisors or investment professionals. They can provide valuable guidance tailored to your financial goals and **risk tolerance**.

What To Do Before Buying Stocks

Set Clear Investment Goals: Determine your investment goals, whether they are long-term wealth accumulation, short-term gains, retirement planning, or any other specific objectives. Understanding your goals will guide your investment decisions.

Assess Your Risk Tolerance: Evaluate your risk tolerance by considering your financial goals, personal circumstances, risk capacity, and risk attitude. This will help determine the level of risk you are comfortable taking on and the types of stocks and investment strategies that align with your risk tolerance.

Educate Yourself: Gain knowledge about stock investing and the financial markets. Understand key investment concepts, such as valuation methods, **fundamental** and **technical analysis**, diversification, and market evaluations. Read books, articles, attend seminars, or take courses to build your knowledge base. It is important to make informed investment decisions.

Create a Budget and Emergency Fund: Establish a budget to determine how much money you can realistically allocate to investing. Ensure you have an emergency fund in place to cover unexpected expenses or financial setbacks. It is crucial not to invest money you cannot afford to lose. As a teenager with less experience with money it is important to work with your parents or guardian during this step.

Define an Investment Strategy: Develop an investment strategy based on your goals, risk tolerance, and time frame. Determine whether you want to focus on individual stocks, **exchange-traded funds (ETFs)**, **mutual funds**, or a combination of these. Decide if you want to be a passive investor or actively manage your portfolio. Your strategy should align with your goals and risk profile.

Choose a Brokerage Account: Select a reputable brokerage firm or an online platform to open an investment account. Consider factors like fees and commissions, ease of use, research tools, customer support, and the range of available investment options. Compare different options to find the brokerage account that suits your needs.

Research and Analyze Stocks: Before purchasing stocks, conduct thorough research and analysis. Study the financial health, performance, and growth prospects of the companies you are interested in. Analyze their financial statements, **earnings reports**, industry trends, and competitive landscape. Consider using both **fundamental analysis** and **technical analysis** to make informed decisions.

Construct a Diversified Portfolio: Diversify your investment portfolio by investing in different companies, sectors, and **asset** classes. This helps to spread risk and reduce the impact of any single stock's performance on your overall portfolio. Consider diversifying across industries, geographies, company sizes, and investment styles.

Determine Entry and Exit Strategies:
Establish criteria for buying and selling
stocks. Decide on the price levels, valuation
metrics, or other indicators that will trigger
your investment decisions. Similarly, define
exit strategies for taking profits, cutting
losses, or rebalancing your portfolio. Having
predetermined rules can prevent emotional
decision-making and assist with disciplined
investing.

Monitor and Review: Continuously
monitor your stocks and regularly review
your investment portfolio. Stay updated
with company news, macroeconomic
factors, industry trends, and market
conditions. Adjust your portfolio as needed,
rebalancing or making strategic changes
based on changing circumstances or your
investment goals.

History Of The Stock Market

The stock market, as we know it today, has evolved
over centuries and its creation can be traced back to
the origins of modern **capitalism**. Here is a brief
overview of how the stock market came into
existence:

The earliest forms of trading stocks can be traced
back to ancient Rome and medieval Europe when

merchants and traders would gather in designated marketplaces to buy and sell shares in businesses or ventures.

In the early 17th century, the Dutch East India Company became one of the first companies to issue shares of stock to the public. These shares were traded on the Amsterdam Stock Exchange, considered the world's first formal stock exchange.

The first recognized stock exchange is generally considered to be the Amsterdam Stock Exchange (now known as Euronext Amsterdam), founded in 1602. It was established by the Dutch East India Company, which issued shares to the public as a means to raise capital for its expeditions and trading ventures.

The Amsterdam Stock Exchange initially operated as an informal market in the courtyard of the Amsterdam Stock Exchange building, known as the Beurs van Hendrick de Keyser. Traders would gather to buy and sell shares of the Dutch East India Company and other ventures, as well as **commodities** like spices. Over time, the exchange grew in prominence and formalized its operations.

The success of the Amsterdam Stock Exchange paved the way for the establishment of other stock exchanges around the world. The London Stock Exchange (founded in 1801) and the New York Stock Exchange (founded in 1792) are among the oldest stock exchanges that followed in the footsteps of the Amsterdam Stock Exchange.

Over time, stock trading shifted from physical trading floors to more formalized settings. In the 18th and 19th centuries, various stock exchanges were established in major cities around the world, such as the London Stock Exchange, New York Stock Exchange, and Paris Bourse.

The Industrial Revolution in the 18th and 19th centuries saw a surge in the creation of companies seeking capital to finance large-scale infrastructure and industrial projects. The stock market developed as a means for these companies to raise funds by issuing shares to investors.

As the stock market grew, regulations were put in place to ensure fair and orderly trading. Governments established regulatory bodies, like the **Securities and Exchange Commission (SEC)** in the United States, to enforce laws and protect investors.

The stock market has undergone significant transformations with the advent of technology. Electronic trading platforms and computerized systems replaced traditional trading floors, enabling faster and more efficient trading.

Today, the stock market is a global network of exchanges where millions of investors trade stocks and other financial instruments. It has become an essential component of modern economic systems, providing companies with access to capital and investors with opportunities to invest and grow their wealth.

Stock Exchanges Explained

A **stock exchange** is a platform where buyers and sellers come together to trade securities or financial instruments such as stocks, bonds, and **derivatives.** Here is an explanation of some prominent stock exchanges:

New York Stock Exchange (NYSE): The NYSE is the largest stock exchange by market capitalization and is located on Wall Street in New York City. It facilitates the trading of equities, Exchange Traded Funds (ETFs), and bonds. The NYSE is known for its iconic trading floor where traders use complex hand signals to communicate.

NASDAQ: The NASDAQ, located in New York City, is the world's second-largest stock exchange. It specializes in the trading of technology companies, such as high-growth startups. Unlike the NYSE, it is a fully electronic exchange with no physical trading floor. NASDAQ is also known for its benchmark stock index, the NASDAQ

Composite Index, which includes popular tech stocks like Apple and Amazon.

London Stock Exchange (LSE): The LSE is the primary stock exchange in the United Kingdom and one of the largest in Europe. It offers a wide range of securities, including equities, fixed-income products, and derivatives. The LSE operates several market platforms, including the Main Market for large, established companies, and the Alternative Investment Market (AIM) for smaller, growth-oriented companies.

Tokyo Stock Exchange (TSE): The TSE is the main stock exchange in Japan. It is one of the world's largest exchanges by market capitalization and provides a marketplace for equities, bonds, ETFs, and investment trusts. The TSE is known for its high liquidity and plays a crucial role in the Japanese economy.

Shanghai Stock Exchange (SSE): The SSE is the primary stock exchange in mainland China, and it has the highest number of listed companies globally. It operates two main trading venues: the Main Board, which includes large companies, and the Science and Technology Innovation Board (STAR Market) for technology-focused firms. The SSE is regulated by the China Securities Regulatory Commission.

Bombay Stock Exchange (BSE): The BSE is the oldest stock exchange in Asia and is located in Mumbai, India. It is one of the leading exchanges in India for equities, derivatives, and currency trading. The BSE operates the Sensex, the benchmark stock index representing the top 30 companies listed on the exchange.

Frankfurt Stock Exchange (FSE): The FSE is the largest stock exchange in Germany and one of the most important in Europe. It offers trading in stocks, bonds, funds, and derivatives. The FSE is known for its flagship indices, such as the DAX (Deutscher Aktienindex), which tracks the performance of the 30 largest and most liquid German companies.

These are just a few examples of stock exchanges, and there are many others around the world, each catering to the trading needs of their respective regions and industries.

Chapter 2: Risk and Diversification

"The biggest risk is not taking any risk. In a world that is changing quickly, the only strategy that is guaranteed to fail is not taking risks." - Mark Zuckerberg

Evaluating Risk Tolerance

A risk is a potential occurrence that may result in harm, loss, or negative consequences. It refers to the uncertainty associated with an action, decision, or event, where there is a possibility of an unfavorable outcome. Risks can arise from various sources, including natural events, human activities, financial transactions, technological failures, or even personal choices. Evaluating and managing risks are essential in order to minimize potential damages and make informed decisions.

It's important to note that investing in stocks involves risk, and there are no guaranteed returns. It is advisable to assess your risk tolerance, conduct thorough research, diversify your portfolio, and consider seeking professional advice if needed to mitigate the risks associated with stock investing.

Assessing your risk tolerance when trading stocks is important to ensure you are comfortable with the level of risk you are taking on. Here are some steps to assess your risk tolerance:

Financial Goals and Time Frames: Consider your financial goals and the **time horizon** for your investments. Are you investing for short-term gains or long-term wealth accumulation? If you have a longer time frame, you may be able to take on more risk, as you have more time to recover from any potential losses.

Personal Circumstances: Evaluate your personal circumstances, such as your age, income, savings, debt levels, and overall financial stability. Younger individuals with stable income and low financial obligations may have a higher risk tolerance, whereas individuals nearing retirement with limited income streams may have a lower risk tolerance.

Risk Capacity: Assess your risk capacity, which is your ability to absorb financial losses without significant negative impact. Consider factors such as your **net worth**, income stability, emergency fund, and other investments. A higher risk capacity allows for a higher risk tolerance.

Risk Attitude: Consider your psychological attitude towards risk. Some individuals are more comfortable taking on higher risks and experiencing volatility in pursuit of potential higher returns, while others may be more **risk-averse** and prioritize capital preservation. Understanding your risk attitude is crucial in determining your risk tolerance.

Risk Assessment Questionnaires: Many financial institutions and online platforms offer risk tolerance questionnaires or assessments that can help gauge your risk tolerance. These questionnaires typically ask about your investment knowledge, risk preferences, investment experience, and reactions to hypothetical scenarios. The results can provide a starting point for understanding your risk tolerance.

Seek Professional Advice: If you are unsure about assessing your risk tolerance independently, consider seeking advice from financial advisors or investment professionals. They can help assess your risk tolerance based on your financial situation, goals, and characteristics, and provide guidance on appropriate investment strategies.

Types of Risk

Remember that risk tolerance is a personal decision and can vary from person to person. It is crucial to be honest with yourself about your risk comfort level and ensure that your investment decisions align with your risk tolerance. Regularly reassessing your risk tolerance is also important as your financial situation, goals, and attitudes may change over time. Stock investing comes with a variety of risks that investors should be aware of. Some of the key risks include:

> **Market Risk:** The value of stocks can fluctuate significantly due to market conditions, economic factors, and investor sentiment. Market risk refers to the potential for losses due to broad market declines or volatility. Factors like recessions, geopolitical events, interest rate changes, or industry-specific issues can lead to market fluctuations and affect stock prices.

> **Company-Specific Risk:** Investing in individual stocks exposes investors to company-specific risks. These risks can include poor management decisions, changes in industry dynamics, product failures, regulatory changes, lawsuits, or financial distress. If a company encounters

any of these issues, it can result in a significant decline in the stock price and potential investment losses.

Liquidity Risk: Liquidity refers to the ease of buying or selling an investment. Some stocks may have low trading volumes or face restrictions on buying or selling, which can make it difficult to enter or exit positions at desired prices. Illiquid stocks may be more costly to buy or sell shares.

Concentration Risk: Concentrating your investments in a few stocks or a specific sector increases the risk of losing a significant portion of your investment if those stocks perform poorly or the sector as a whole experiences setbacks. Diversification can help **mitigate** concentration risk.

Currency Risk: If you invest in stocks outside your home currency, fluctuations in currency exchange rates can impact your returns. **Exchange rate** movements can increase or decrease your investment gains or losses when you convert your investments back to your home currency.

Political and Regulatory Risk: Changes in government policies, regulations, or political stability can impact the performance of stocks. This risk is particularly relevant when investing in foreign stocks or in industries that are influenced by government policies, such as healthcare, energy, or telecommunications.

Timing Risk: Trying to time the market and make investment decisions based on short-term market movements can be risky. Timing the market consistently and accurately is extremely difficult, and attempting to do so can lead to missed opportunities or losses.

Portfolio Diversification

Diversification of a portfolio refers to the practice of investing in a variety of different assets or securities in order to spread out risk and potentially increase potential returns. By including a mix of asset classes, industries, geographic locations, and investment types, diversification aims to minimize the impact of any one investment performing poorly and increase the likelihood of some investments performing well.

The basic principle of diversification is that not all investments will perform in the same way or at the same time. Different asset classes, such as stocks, bonds, commodities, or **real estate**, have varying risk and return profiles. Therefore, when one investment is underperforming, others may still be generating positive returns, reducing the overall impact of any single investment on the portfolio.

Diversification can be achieved at different levels. For example, it can involve spreading investments across different companies within one industry or across various industries. It can also involve investing in assets across multiple countries or regions to reduce exposure to any one country's economic conditions or political events. Additionally, diversification can be achieved by investing in different types of securities, such as stocks, bonds, mutual funds, exchange-traded funds (ETFs), or alternative investments.

The goal of diversification is not to eliminate all risk but to manage or reduce it. While diversification can help mitigate the potential downside, it may also limit the upside as not all investments will perform exceptionally well in favorable market conditions. Determining the right level of diversification depends on an individual's risk tolerance, investment goals, and time horizon. It is generally recommended to work with a financial advisor to develop a diversified portfolio that aligns with one's specific needs and circumstances.

People diversify their stock portfolios for several reasons, including risk reduction, potential for higher returns, and protection against market volatility. Here are the key reasons why individuals diversify their stock portfolios:

Risk reduction: By spreading investments across different stocks and sectors, investors can reduce the risk of substantial losses. Diversification helps mitigate the impact of poor performance or negative events affecting a single stock or a particular industry. If one investment underperforms, potential losses may be offset by the performance of other investments.

Potential for higher returns: Diversification allows investors to allocate their funds across various stocks with different growth prospects. While some stocks may experience poor performance, others could deliver significant gains. A well-diversified portfolio provides the opportunity to capture upside potential from different investments, potentially leading to higher overall returns.

Protection against market volatility: Stock markets can be volatile; prices can fluctuate dramatically in response to economic events, **geopolitical** tensions, or company-specific news. By diversifying their portfolios, investors can minimize the impact of individual stock price swings or market downturns. This way, if one stock or sector experiences significant decline, the overall impact on the portfolio may be less severe.

Preservation of capital: Diversification is a risk management strategy aimed at preserving capital and minimizing losses. By avoiding overexposure to a single stock or sector, investors reduce the potential for substantial capital erosion in case of unexpected negative events. The goal is to limit the downside risk and protect the portfolio's overall value.

Exposure to different market opportunities: Diversification allows investors to participate in different market opportunities across various sectors and regions. By investing in a range of companies and industries, investors can take advantage of growth potential in different segments of the economy. This broad exposure can provide access to emerging trends, technological advancements, or sectors that may outperform others.

It's important to note that diversification does not completely eliminate risk, but rather spreads it across different investments. Proper diversification involves carefully selecting a mix of stocks with varying characteristics, such as market capitalization, industry, and risk profiles.

How To Achieve Portfolio Diversification

Diversifying a stock portfolio involves spreading investments across different stocks, sectors, and potentially other asset classes. Here are several ways to achieve diversification:

Invest in different sectors: Allocate funds across various sectors of the economy, such as technology, healthcare, finance, **consumer goods**, and energy. Different sectors tend to perform differently at various stages of the economic cycle, so diversifying across sectors helps balance risk and potential returns.

Choose stocks of different market capitalizations: Invest in companies of different sizes, including large-cap (well-established companies), mid-cap (medium-sized companies), and small-cap (smaller, potentially higher-growth companies). Companies of different sizes often respond differently to market conditions, providing diversification benefits.

Consider geographic diversification: Invest in stocks of companies located in different regions and countries. This helps protect your portfolio from localized economic or political risks. Accessing international markets enables exposure to different economies, industries, and currencies.

Include dividend-paying stocks: Dividend-paying stocks can provide a consistent income stream, even during market downturns. Consider including stocks with a track record of paying **dividends** or investing in dividend-focused funds.

Allocate a portion to bonds or other asset classes: Diversify beyond stocks by including **bonds**, exchange-traded funds (ETFs), **real estate investment trusts (REITs),** or other investment vehicles. Bonds generally have a lower correlation to stocks and can help stabilize a portfolio during market volatility.

Regularly rebalance your portfolio: Maintain a disciplined approach to portfolio management by periodically reviewing and rebalancing your investments. This involves selling assets that have performed poorly and investing in those that are performing well. Rebalancing ensures your portfolio remains aligned with your desired asset allocation and diversification goals.

Consider using index funds or ETFs:
Invest in low-cost index funds or
exchange-traded funds that track broad
market indices. These funds offer instant
diversification by providing exposure to a
basket of stocks or bonds, replicating the
performance of the underlying index.

**Conduct thorough research and
analysis:** Before investing in any stock or
asset, conduct detailed research and
analysis to understand the company's
financials, competitive positioning, future
prospects, and potential risks. Diversifying a
portfolio does not mean investing blindly; it
requires making informed investment
decisions.

Remember that diversification does not guarantee
profits or protect against losses. It's important to
find the right balance based on your investment
goals, risk tolerance, and time horizon. Consulting
with a **financial advisor** can provide personalized
guidance on how to effectively diversify your stock
portfolio.

Chapter 3: Getting Started: Brokerage Accounts And Investment Strategies

"The stock market is filled with individuals who know the price of everything, but the value of nothing." – Philip Fisher

Brokerage Accounts

A brokerage account is a type of financial account that allows an individual or entity to buy and sell various financial securities, such as stocks, bonds, mutual funds, exchange-traded funds (ETFs), options, and other investment products. It acts as an intermediary between an investor and the financial markets.

Here are some key features of a brokerage account:

Access to Financial Markets: A brokerage account provides investors with access to various financial markets, including stock exchanges and bond markets, where they can trade and invest in a wide range of securities.

Buying and Selling of Securities: With a brokerage account, you can place orders to buy or sell securities through the brokerage firm's trading platform or by contacting a broker directly. The transactions are executed on your behalf in the market.

Custody and Safekeeping: When you purchase securities through a brokerage account, they are held in custody by the brokerage firm on your behalf. This ensures the safekeeping of your investments.

Account Management: Brokerage accounts provide tools and resources for investors to manage their portfolios. This includes access to research materials, real-time market data, investment analysis, and performance tracking.

Margin Trading: Some brokerage accounts allow investors to trade on margin, which means borrowing money from the brokerage firm to buy securities. Margin trading can amplify potential returns but also increases risk, as losses can exceed the initial investment.

Fees and Commissions: Brokerage firms charge fees and commissions for executing trades and providing various services. These typically include transaction fees, account maintenance fees, and management fees,

among others. The fee structure can vary
depending on the brokerage and the type of
account.

It's important to note that brokerage accounts can
be opened with traditional full-service brokerage
firms, online brokerages, or **robo-advisors**. Each
type of brokerage may offer different features,
services, and levels of support, so it's advisable to
research and compare options before choosing a
brokerage account that suits your investment goals
and preferences. Additionally, it's common to link a
bank account or provide funds to the brokerage
account in order to facilitate seamless buying and
selling of securities.

Choosing A Brokerage

Selecting the correct brokerage account tailored to
your specific needs and preferences can greatly
impact your investment performance, costs, and
overall investing experience. Assessing and
comparing different options before making a
decision is important in order to make the most
informed choice. Here are some factors to consider
when selecting a stock brokerage:

> **Fees and Commissions:** Compare the fee
> structure of different brokerage firms. Look
> for low account maintenance fees, trading
> commissions, and other charges that may be
> applicable. However, keep in mind that

some brokers may offer additional services or research tools that justify higher fees.

Account Types and Minimums: Determine the type of account you need, such as individual, joint, retirement (IRA), or custodial accounts. Check if the brokerage offers the desired type of account and confirm whether there are any minimum balance requirements or account opening deposits.

Trading Platform and Tools: Evaluate the brokerage's trading platform and research tools. Look for an intuitive and user-friendly platform that offers real-time quotes, charts, news updates, and technical analysis tools. Advanced features like screening tools and backtesting capabilities can be beneficial for active traders.

Investment Options: Consider the range of investment options offered by the brokerage. Ensure they provide access to the types of investments you are interested in, such as stocks, bonds, mutual funds, ETFs, options, futures, or international securities. Some brokerages may also offer access to IPOs, **fractional shares**, or robo-advisory services.

Customer Support: Assess the quality and availability of customer support. Look for a brokerage that offers multiple channels of customer service, such as phone, email, live chat, or in-person support. Quick and responsive customer support can be crucial when dealing with technical issues or seeking assistance with account-related queries.

Research and Educational Resources: Check if the brokerage provides research reports, market analysis, educational resources, and investment insights. Look for tools and resources that can enhance your understanding of the markets, aid in stock selection, and support your investment decisions.

Mobile and Online Access: Consider the availability and functionality of mobile and online platforms. Ensure that the brokerage provides a mobile app or a responsive website that allows you to trade on the go, access account information, monitor portfolio performance, or receive real-time market updates.

Security and Account Protection: Ensure that the brokerage has robust security measures in place to protect your personal and financial information. Look for brokers that offer advanced encryption, two-factor authentication, and clear policies on data privacy. Verify if the brokerage is a member of the Securities Investor Protection Corporation (SIPC), which provides limited protection for customers in the event of brokerage compromise.

Reputation and Reviews: Research the brokerage's reputation and read reviews from current or past customers. Look for feedback on aspects like reliability, transparency, execution speed, order handling, and overall customer satisfaction. Online forums, industry publications, and independent review sites can provide valuable insights.

Additional Services: Consider any additional services or features offered by the brokerage that align with your needs. This might include access to IPOs, retirement planning tools, educational events, investment advisory services, or access to a network of financial professionals.

By considering these factors and aligning them with your investment goals and preferences, you can choose a stock brokerage that best suits your needs. It is often helpful to compare multiple brokerages, read fine print, and even consider trying out demo accounts or taking advantage of trial periods to get

a firsthand experience before making a final
decision.

Commonly Used Brokerages

The most commonly used brokerages today vary
depending on the region and individual
preferences. However, some of the popular
brokerages that are widely used by investors and
traders include:

Fidelity Investments: Fidelity is a
well-established brokerage that offers a
wide range of investment options, research
tools, and retirement planning services. It
has a user-friendly trading platform and
provides access to stocks, bonds, mutual
funds, ETFs, options, and more.

Charles Schwab: Charles Schwab is
known for its low-cost brokerage services
and robust platform. It offers a variety of
investment options and has recently
eliminated trading commissions for U.S.
stocks, ETFs, and options. It also provides a
wide array of research and educational
resources.

TD Ameritrade: TD Ameritrade is a
leading brokerage with a powerful trading
platform and extensive research tools. It
offers a broad range of investment options,

including stocks, ETFs, mutual funds, options, futures, and forex. TD Ameritrade also provides access to robo-advisory services.

E*TRADE: E*TRADE is a popular brokerage known for its user-friendly interface and comprehensive trading tools. It offers a diverse range of investment options, including stocks, ETFs, mutual funds, bonds, options, and futures. E*TRADE provides in-depth research and analysis, as well as educational resources for investors.

Robinhood: Robinhood gained popularity for its commission-free trading and user-friendly mobile app. It offers a simplified trading experience primarily focused on stocks and ETFs, with limited research tools. Robinhood is particularly popular among younger and **novice** investors.

Interactive Brokers: Interactive Brokers is a brokerage that caters to active and advanced traders. It provides a robust trading platform with advanced tools and offers a wide range of investment options, including stocks, bonds, mutual funds, options, **futures**, and **forex**. Interactive

Brokers is known for its low commissions and extensive global market access.

Vanguard: Vanguard is primarily known for its low-cost index fund offerings, but it also provides brokerage services. It offers commission-free trading for Vanguard mutual funds and ETFs, with competitive fees for other investments. Vanguard focuses on long-term investing and retirement planning.

TradeStation: TradeStation is a brokerage popular among active traders due to its advanced trading tools and customizable platform. It offers access to various investment options, including stocks, ETFs, options, futures, and forex. TradeStation provides a wide range of technical analysis and charting tools.

Webull: Webull offers commission-free trading, allowing users to buy and sell stocks, ETFs, and options without incurring any trading fees. This feature can be attractive to active traders who frequently make trades and want to save on transaction costs. It also allows for paper trading and offers extended trading hours.

Remember, these are just some of the commonly used brokerages, and each firm has its strengths and weaknesses. It is crucial to research and compare various brokerages based on your specific needs and preferences before selecting one.

Types of Brokerage Accounts

There are several different types of brokerage accounts available to investors, depending on their investment goals, financial situation, and preferences. Some common types of brokerage accounts include:

Individual Brokerage Account: This is the most common type of brokerage account and is opened by individuals for personal investment purposes. Individual brokerage accounts allow investors to buy and sell a wide range of financial instruments, such as stocks, bonds, mutual funds, ETFs, and more. They provide flexibility and control over investment decisions.

Joint Brokerage Account: A joint brokerage account is opened by two or more individuals, typically spouses or business partners. It allows all account holders to contribute funds and make investment decisions jointly. Joint brokerage accounts can be useful for managing shared investments or for tax planning purposes.

Retirement Accounts: There are several types of retirement accounts offered by brokerage firms, such as Individual Retirement Accounts (IRAs) and **401(k) accounts.** These accounts offer tax advantages and are designed specifically for retirement savings. Contributions to these accounts may be **tax-deductible** (in traditional IRAs and 401(k)s) or tax-free (in Roth IRAs) depending on the account type.

Margin Accounts: Margin accounts are brokerage accounts that allow investors to borrow money from the broker to buy securities. With a margin account, investors can increase their buying power and potentially amplify their returns. However, margin trading carries additional risks, as losses can be magnified, and **interest** is charged on the borrowed funds.

Custodial Accounts: Custodial accounts are opened by an adult on behalf of a minor, typically their child or grandchild. The custodian manages the account and makes investment decisions until the minor reaches a specified age (usually 18 or 21). Custodial accounts can be used for gifting and teaching financial responsibility to minors.

Managed Accounts: Managed accounts are offered by brokerage firms or investment advisors who manage the investments on behalf of the **account holder**. The investment decisions are made by the professional, based on the account holder's investment goals, risk tolerance, and other preferences. Managed accounts can be tailored to specific investment strategies, such as growth, income, or balanced portfolios.

A **cash account** at a brokerage is a type of brokerage account where all **transactions** are settled in cash. In a cash account, the investor must have sufficient funds or cash equivalents in the account to cover the cost of buying securities. When selling securities, the proceeds from the sale are deposited into the cash account. Key features of a cash account at a brokerage include:

No Margin Trading: Cash accounts do not allow investors to borrow money from the broker to purchase securities. All transactions in a cash account must be made using cash on hand.

No Short Selling: Similarly, short selling (selling securities that you don't own in the anticipation of buying them back at a lower price) is not permitted in cash accounts.

Cash Settled: When buying securities, the funds to cover the transaction must be available in the cash account at the time of the purchase. Likewise, when selling securities, the proceeds from the sale are deposited as cash in the account.

No Interest Charges: Since no borrowing is allowed in cash accounts, there are no interest charges on borrowed funds.

Cash accounts are often suitable for conservative investors who prefer to invest with their own funds without borrowing from the broker. **Pattern day trading (PDT)** rules in the United States require traders to maintain a minimum account balance of $25,000 in order to make more than three day trades within a five-day rolling period. However, using a cash account instead of a margin account can help traders avoid these PDT restrictions. Using a cash account to avoid pattern day trading (PDT) restrictions can be a suitable option for traders who don't meet the $25,000 minimum account balance requirement. However, it's essential to consider the limitations of cash accounts, such as the delay in accessing funds from sold securities and the inability to use margin for leverage. As transactions are settled in cash, there is no risk of margin calls or additional interest expenses. It is important to note that cash accounts may have less buying power compared to margin accounts, where investors can trade on borrowed funds.

It's essential to understand the **terms and conditions** of a cash account and the restrictions it places on trading activities before opening one at a brokerage.

It's important to consider the fees, minimum investment requirements, account features, and other factors when choosing a brokerage account. Different brokerage firms may offer different account types and have varying services and features, so it's advisable to research and compare options before opening an account.

Choosing an Investment Strategy

Choosing an investment strategy provides direction, helps manage risk, maintains consistency, maximizes returns, allows for monitoring and **adaptability**, and optimizes time. It is a crucial step towards achieving financial goals and building long-term wealth. Investing for income and investing for growth are two different strategies with distinct objectives. Here's a breakdown of the key differences:

Investing for Income:
Investing for income focuses on generating a consistent stream of income from investments, such as dividends, interest payments, or rental income. The primary goal is to generate regular

cash flow to meet current income needs. Here are some key characteristics:

Asset Allocation: Investments for income often involve assets that provide regular income, such as dividend-paying stocks, bonds, real estate investment trusts (REITs), or **fixed-income securities**.

Investment Selection: Investors typically look for stable and established companies that have a history of paying dividends and generating consistent income. They may also focus on high-yield bonds or real estate properties that generate regular rental income.

Risk and Volatility: Investments for income tend to prioritize stability and income generation over **capital appreciation**. As a result, these investments may be less volatile compared to growth-oriented investments, but they may come with lower potential for long-term capital growth.

Reinvestment: Income generated from investments can be reinvested or used to cover living expenses and supplement cash flow needs.

Investing for Growth:

Investing for growth, on the other hand, aims to increase the value of investments over the long term. The primary goal is to accumulate wealth by seeking capital appreciation. Here are some key characteristics:

Asset Allocation: Growth-oriented investments typically involve assets with higher growth potential, such as stocks of companies in sectors expected to expand rapidly or emerging markets. Growth-focused investors may also consider high-growth industries like technology or innovation.

Investment Selection: Investors often focus on companies or funds that have a track record of strong revenue and earnings growth. They look for businesses with potential for market share expansion, new product developments, or significant industry advancements.

Risk and Volatility: Growth-oriented investments generally involve higher levels of risk and volatility compared to income-focused investments. This is because growth stocks can experience larger fluctuations in price due to changes in investor sentiment or market conditions.

Reinvestment: In growth investing, reinvesting profits back into the investment is a common strategy to compound returns over time and benefit from the power of compounding.

Ultimately, whether an investor chooses income or growth investing depends on their financial goals, risk tolerance, time horizon, and individual circumstances. Some investors may prefer a combination of both strategies to achieve a balance between income and capital appreciation. It is important to evaluate your own financial objectives and consult with a financial advisor to create an investment strategy that aligns with your specific needs.

Investment Strategies

There are various investment strategies that investors can employ depending on their goals, risk tolerance, and investment horizon. Here are some common investment strategies:

Buy and Hold: This strategy involves buying securities and holding them for the long term, regardless of short-term market fluctuations. Investors who believe in the fundamental strength of their investments often follow this strategy, focusing on the long-term growth potential.

Value Investing: Value investors look for stocks that they believe are undervalued by the market. They typically seek companies with strong fundamentals, such as low price-to-earnings ratio, low price-to-book ratio, or high dividend yield. The idea is to buy these stocks at a discount and hold them until the market recognizes their true value.

Growth Investing: Growth investors focus on companies that show strong growth potential in terms of revenue, earnings, and market share. They invest in companies operating in expanding industries and aim to profit from the stock's price appreciation over time.

Dividend Investing: Dividend investors prioritize stocks that pay regular dividends. They focus on companies with a history of consistently increasing dividend payments. This strategy aims to generate income through dividend payments, along with potential capital appreciation.

Index Investing: Index investors seek to replicate the performance of a specific market index, such as the **S&P 500** or the **FTSE 100**. They invest in index funds or exchange-traded funds (ETFs) that track the chosen index, providing diversified market exposure at a low cost.

Momentum Investing: Momentum investors look for stocks that are experiencing positive price movements, aiming to ride the upward trend. They focus on stocks that are showing momentum indicators like strong price performance or increasing trading volume.

Contrarian Investing: Contrarian investors go against market sentiment, buying stocks that are out of favor or undervalued. They believe that markets tend to overreact to news or events, presenting opportunities to buy stocks at a lower price than their intrinsic value.

Sector Rotation: Sector rotation involves actively shifting investments between different sectors depending on economic conditions. Investors aim to benefit from sectors that are expected to outperform and avoid those that may underperform in different stages of the economic cycle.

It's important to note that each strategy comes with its own risks and potential rewards. It is advisable to thoroughly understand the strategy, conduct research, and diversify investments to manage risk effectively. Consulting with a financial advisor can also provide personalized guidance based on individual circumstances.

Day Trading vs Swing trading

Day trading is a short-term trading strategy where traders buy and sell financial instruments (such as stocks, currencies, or commodities) within the same trading day. Day traders attempt to profit from the intraday price movements, taking advantage of volatility and short-term trends. Day traders often use leverage and trade with high volume to amplify potential gains.

Characteristics of day trading include:

Holding Period: Day traders close all their positions by the end of the trading day and do not hold positions overnight.

Frequency of Trades: Day traders typically execute multiple trades throughout the day, sometimes within minutes or seconds, aiming to capture small price movements.

Technical Analysis: Day traders heavily rely on technical analysis tools, charts, and patterns to identify short-term price trends, support and resistance levels, and potential entry and exit points.

Margin Trading: Day traders often use margin accounts provided by their brokers, allowing them to trade with borrowed money. This leverage amplifies both potential gains and losses.

Active Monitoring: Day trading requires continuous monitoring of price movements, news, and market conditions. Traders need to react quickly to changing market dynamics and execute trades timely.

Swing trading is a medium-term trading strategy that aims to capture price swings or "swings" within a trending market. Swing traders hold their positions for more than a day, typically several days to weeks, allowing them to take advantage of short-term price fluctuations.

Characteristics of swing trading include:

Holding Period: Swing traders hold positions for a longer duration compared to day traders. They aim to capture the price movement during a swing within an established trend.

Trend Identification: Swing traders identify trends in the market and look for potential entry and exit points within that trend. They attempt to buy near the bottom of a swing **(support)** and sell near the top **(resistance)**.

Technical Analysis: Swing traders primarily rely on technical analysis, using tools like trendlines, moving averages, and oscillators to identify trends, support and resistance levels, and potential reversals.

Risk Management: Swing traders often use stop-loss orders to manage risk and protect profits. These orders automatically sell the position if the price moves against them beyond a predetermined level.

Less Active Monitoring: Swing trading requires less monitoring compared to day trading as it focuses on capturing intermediate price movements. Traders do not need to be constantly engaged in front of the market.

Both day trading and swing trading carry risks, such as the potential for losses due to market volatility and the risk of making emotional or impulsive trading decisions. It is important for traders to have a well-defined trading plan, risk management strategy, and sufficient knowledge and experience before engaging in these trading strategies.

Goals of Different Investors

The specific goals of stock traders can vary based on individual strategies, preferences, and risk tolerance. However, the overarching goal for most stock traders is to generate profits from their trades by capitalizing on price fluctuations in the stock market. Here are some common goals that stock traders may have:

Capital appreciation: Traders aim to buy stocks at a lower price and sell them at a higher price, generating a profit from the price difference. They seek to identify undervalued stocks or take advantage of short-term price movements to maximize capital appreciation.

Risk management: Traders often employ risk management strategies to protect their capital and minimize potential losses. This may involve setting stop-loss orders to automatically sell a stock if it reaches a predetermined price level, diversifying their portfolio to spread risk, or using hedging techniques to offset potential losses.

Consistent returns: Traders may aim for consistent and steady returns over time, rather than relying on occasional large gains. They may opt for strategies like swing trading or day trading to take advantage of short-term price fluctuations and generate smaller, frequent profits.

Beating market benchmarks: Some traders strive to outperform recognized market benchmarks, such as stock market indices (e.g., S&P 500 or **Dow Jones Industrial Average**). This goal often involves thorough research, active portfolio management, and identifying opportunities that can generate higher returns than the overall market.

Long-term wealth building: Traders may also have a long-term goal of building wealth through successful stock trading. In this case, they may focus on fundamental analysis to identify fundamentally strong companies with growth potential and hold their investments for an extended period to benefit from capital appreciation.

It's important to note that trading in the stock market involves inherent risks, and individual goals and strategies may vary significantly. Some traders may have short-term goals centered on quick profits, while others have long-term investment goals oriented toward wealth accumulation.

Chapter 4: Market Evaluation

"Wall Street is the only place that people ride to work in a Rolls Royce to get advice from those who take the subway." - Warren Buffett

Market evaluation refers to the process of assessing and analyzing various factors that influence the overall performance and outlook of a particular market or industry. It involves gathering and analyzing relevant data to determine the attractiveness, potential risks, and opportunities within a market.

Here are a few key components of market evaluation:

Market Size and Growth: Evaluating the size and growth rate of a market helps to assess its potential. This involves analyzing factors such as population trends, consumer behavior, economic indicators, and industry reports to determine the market's current and future size.

Market Trends: Understanding market trends is crucial for identifying emerging opportunities and threats. Evaluating trends can involve analyzing changes in consumer preferences, technological advancements and competition within the market.

Competitive Landscape: Assessing the competitive landscape involves analyzing the key players, their market shares, strategies, and strengths. This analysis helps to evaluate the intensity of competition and the overall market structure.

Customer Analysis: Understanding target customers is essential to assess demand and market positioning. This involves analyzing consumer demographics, behavior, needs, and preferences through market research, surveys, and customer feedback.

SWOT Analysis: Conducting a SWOT (Strengths, Weaknesses, Opportunities, Threats) analysis helps in evaluating the market's internal and external factors. By identifying strengths and weaknesses, businesses can leverage their competitive advantages and address areas requiring improvement. Additionally, opportunities and threats help identify potential avenues for growth and key risks that may impact the market.

Economic and Political Factors:
Assessing economic and political factors
helps to understand the macro environment
and its influence on the market. Factors
such as **GDP growth**, **inflation rates**,
interest rates, government policies, and
regulations can significantly impact
market conditions and investment
opportunities.

Market Forecasting: Estimating future
market conditions is a critical part of market
evaluation. This involves using historical
data, industry trends, and expert insights to
make predictions about market growth,
demand, and potential challenges.

Market evaluation plays a crucial role in various
areas, such as market entry decisions, investment
planning, product development, and strategy
formulation. It helps businesses and investors make
informed decisions by understanding the market
dynamics, risks, and opportunities associated with
a particular industry or market segment.

Crashes vs Corrections

A stock market crash and a stock market correction
are two different types of significant declines in the
overall stock market. Here's an explanation of each:

A **stock market crash** is an abrupt and severe decline in stock prices that happens relatively quickly, usually over a few days or weeks. It is often characterized by panic selling and a rapid drop in market indices, such as the S&P 500 or Dow Jones Industrial Average. Stock market crashes are usually accompanied by widespread investor fear, increased volatility, and a significant loss of wealth. Crashes are typically caused by major market-wide events, such as financial crises, economic recessions, or severe geopolitical events. Examples of historical stock market crashes include the Great Depression crash in 1929, the Black Monday crash in 1987, and the Global Financial Crisis crash in 2008.

A **stock market correction** is a less severe decline in stock prices that occurs after a significant and prolonged period of market gains. It is a natural and healthy part of the market cycle, serving to correct market excesses and bring stock prices back to more reasonable levels. Corrections are typically characterized by a decline of 10% to 20% from recent market highs. Unlike crashes, corrections are often less abrupt and more gradual, taking place over several weeks or months. Corrections can occur due to various factors, such as an economic slowdown, concerns over interest rates or inflation, geopolitical tensions, or market valuation concerns. Examples of stock market corrections include the Dotcom Bubble burst in 2000 and the more recent COVID-19-induced correction in early 2020.

While both stock market crashes and corrections involve significant declines in stock prices, crashes are usually far more severe, rapid, and have a more profound impact on the overall economy. Corrections, on the other hand, are considered a normal part of the market cycle and are often seen as opportunities for long-term investors to buy stocks at more attractive prices.

Bull Market vs Bear Market

A **bull market** is a term used to describe a financial market that experiences a sustained upward trend in prices over an extended period. It signifies a period of optimism, investor confidence, and overall market growth. In a bull market, the demand for stocks exceeds the supply, leading to rising stock prices. Here are some key characteristics and factors associated with bull markets:

> **Rising stock prices:** Bull markets are characterized by a consistent increase in the prices of stocks or other financial assets. This upward trend is often driven by positive investor sentiment, strong

economic indicators, and improving corporate earnings.

Investor optimism: Bull markets are usually accompanied by high levels of investor optimism and confidence in the future prospects of the market. Positive news regarding economic performance, industry growth, or government policies can fuel this optimism and encourage investors to buy stocks.

Increased trading volume: As more investors participate in a bull market, trading volume tends to rise. This increased activity reflects heightened market interest, as more buyers enter the market to take advantage of the upward trend.

Broad-based market growth: Bull markets typically witness overall market growth, where a majority of stocks or sectors experience rising prices. It is common for indices, such as the S&P 500 or Dow Jones Industrial Average, to reach new all-time highs during a bull market.

Favorable economic conditions: A bull market often coincides with a period of strong economic growth, low unemployment rates, and stable inflation. Positive economic indicators, such as rising

GDP, low-interest rates, or **robust** consumer spending, contribute to investor confidence and result in market optimism.

Potential for higher returns: Bull markets can provide opportunities for investors to earn higher returns on their investments. As stock prices rise, investors who have bought securities earlier may see their holdings appreciate in value, leading to capital gains.

It's important to note that bull markets are not indefinite and can come to an end. Economic downturns, policy changes, geopolitical factors, or unexpected events can cause a shift in market sentiment and mark the transition to a bear market, characterized by falling stock prices and pessimism. Therefore, investors should carefully assess market conditions, monitor indicators, and manage their portfolios accordingly during bull markets, recognizing that cycles of up and down markets are a natural part of the investing landscape.

A **bear market** refers to a period of time in financial markets when stock prices experience a sustained decline or prolonged period of negative performance. It is characterized by **pessimism**, investor caution, and a general downturn in market sentiment. Here are some key characteristics and factors associated with bear markets:

Falling stock prices: In a bear market, stock prices generally decline across the board or in specific sectors or indices. This downward trend is often caused by factors such as economic **recession**, negative news, poor corporate earnings, or deteriorating market conditions.

Investor pessimism: Bear markets are typified by widespread pessimism and a lack of investor confidence. Negative economic indicators, uncertainty, or geopolitical events can erode investor sentiment, leading to increased selling pressure and a decline in demand for stocks.

Decreased trading volume: As investor confidence wanes during a bear market, trading volume typically decreases. Anticipating further market declines, investors may reduce their trading activity and hold onto their existing investments, leading to lower trading volumes overall.

Sector-specific declines: While a bear market often encompasses a broad decline in stock prices, it is possible to see sectors or industries experience more significant declines than others. Economic factors or industry-specific issues can contribute to further weakness in certain sectors during a bear market.

Economic downturns: Bear markets are often associated with broader economic downturns or recessions. Factors such as rising unemployment rates, declining GDP, weakening consumer spending, or higher interest rates can contribute to the negative sentiment and downward pressure on stock prices.

Potential for increased volatility: Volatility tends to increase during bear markets, as prices fluctuate more dramatically and swings in market sentiment become more pronounced. Investors may experience heightened uncertainty and face difficult decisions as market conditions remain unstable.

Possibility for defensive strategies: During bear markets, investors may employ defensive strategies to minimize losses or protect capital. These strategies can include holding more cash or cash equivalents, shifting investments to more defensive sectors (e.g., utilities or consumer staples), or utilizing **hedging** techniques to offset potential losses.

It's important to note that bear markets are temporary and eventually give way to new bull market cycles. While investing during bear markets presents challenges, it can also offer opportunities to purchase quality stocks at lower prices when market valuations are depressed. However, timing market bottoms and rebounds is inherently difficult, and investors should exercise caution and conduct appropriate research before making investment decisions during bear market conditions.

Stock Prices

Stock prices are driven by a variety of factors that influence supply and demand in the market. Here are some key drivers of stock prices:

> **Company Performance:** Stock prices are fundamentally linked to the performance and financial health of the underlying company. Factors such as revenue growth, earnings, profitability, and competitive positioning can significantly impact stock prices. Positive performance may lead to increased investor confidence and demand for the stock, driving its price higher.

> **Economic Factors:** Economic conditions, such as GDP growth, interest rates, inflation, and **employment** levels, can impact stock prices. Positive economic indicators generally create a favorable environment for businesses, leading to

increased investor optimism and higher stock prices.

Industry and Sector Trends: Stocks within specific industries or sectors can be influenced by trends and developments affecting that particular area of the market. Factors like technological advancements, regulatory changes, and market disruptions may impact the performance of companies within a sector, ultimately affecting their stock prices.

Investor Sentiment and Market Psychology: Investor **sentiment** and market psychology play a significant role in driving stock prices. Positive sentiment, fueled by **optimism**, can drive stock prices higher, while negative sentiment can lead to selling pressure and price declines. Factors like market speculation, news, and geopolitical events can influence investor sentiment and the overall market mood.

Supply and Demand Dynamics: The basic economic principle of supply and demand applies to stocks as well. When there is high demand for a stock and limited supply, the price tends to increase. Conversely, when there is a higher supply of shares and limited demand, the price may decrease.

Analyst Recommendations and News: Analyst recommendations, earnings reports, news releases, and other market-related information can impact stock prices. Positive news or favorable analyst opinions about a company can attract more buyers, driving up the stock price. Similarly, negative news or analyst downgrades can lead to selling pressure and price declines.

Market Manipulation and Speculation: While illegal, market manipulation and speculative trading can temporarily impact stock prices. Activities like **pump and dump schemes**, insider trading, and short-term speculative trading can artificially inflate or deflate stock prices, deviating from their intrinsic value.

It's important to note that stock prices are dynamic and can be influenced by a combination of these factors. Therefore, understanding and evaluating multiple factors is crucial for investors in order to make informed investment decisions.

Stock Price Movement

While stock price movement is influenced by numerous factors and is difficult to predict with certainty, here are some possible signals that could indicate a potential increase in stock price:

Positive Earnings Report: A company's positive earnings report, exceeding market expectations, can often lead to an increase in stock price as it suggests the company is performing well.

Strong Revenue Growth: Consistent revenue growth demonstrates the company's ability to generate higher sales, which may lead to increased investor confidence and a subsequent rise in stock price.

Increased Profit Margins: Improvements in profit margins indicate that a company is becoming more efficient in managing costs and generating higher profits, potentially leading to a stock price increase.

Positive Analyst Recommendations: When influential analysts or research institutions issue positive recommendations or upgrade the stock's rating, it often encourages investors to buy, potentially pushing up the stock price.

Favorable Industry Trends: If a company operates in an industry experiencing positive trends or supportive market conditions, it may suggest that the company's stock price has the potential to increase alongside industry growth.

New Product Launch or Innovation: Companies that develop and launch successful new products or innovative solutions often attract investor interest and confidence, potentially contributing to a rise in stock price.

Increased Institutional Buying: When institutional investors such as mutual funds or pension funds increase their holdings in a stock, it can indicate positive sentiment and potential price appreciation as these institutions often conduct thorough research before investing.

Positive Macro-economic Indicators: Favorable macroeconomic indicators, such as low unemployment rates, strong GDP growth, or positive consumer sentiment, can impact the overall stock market positively and potentially result in a rise in stock prices across various sectors.

Bullish Technical Indicators: Traders who use technical analysis may identify specific chart patterns or indicators suggesting bullish market trends, such as higher highs, higher lows, moving average crossovers, or breakouts, signaling a potential stock price increase.

Positive News or Catalysts: Any positive news related to a company, such as strategic partnerships, new contracts, regulatory approvals, or merger and acquisition activity, can boost investor confidence and act as a catalyst for stock price appreciation.

It's essential to note that these signals do not guarantee a stock price increase, as the market is influenced by various factors, including investor sentiment, geopolitical events, and market volatility. Thorough research and analysis should always be conducted before making investment decisions.

Here are some warning signs that could indicate a potential decline in a stock's price:

Negative Earnings Report: If a company reports lower than expected earnings or experiences consistent declines in profitability, it may create concerns for investors and potentially lead to a decline in the stock price.

Declining Revenue: A company's consistent decline in revenue can be worrisome as it suggests a potential decrease in sales and market share, which could impact investor confidence and lead to a stock price decline.

Decreased Profit Margins: If a company's profit margins are shrinking over time, it may indicate challenges in managing costs or facing increased competition, potentially leading to a decline in the stock's price.

Negative Analyst Recommendations: When influential analysts or research institutions issue negative recommendations or downgrade a stock's rating, it often discourages investors from buying, potentially pushing the stock price down.

Unfavorable Industry Trends: If a company operates in an industry experiencing negative trends or challenging market conditions, it may suggest that the company's stock price could decline alongside industry deterioration.

Product Failures or Recalls: Companies that experience significant product failures, recalls, or reputational damage could face a decline in investor confidence, leading to a potential decrease in stock price.

Insider Selling: When company insiders, such as **executives** or **board members**, sell large amounts of their shares in the company, it is often seen as a negative signal by investors, potentially leading to a decline in the stock's price.

Bearish Technical Indicators: Traders who use technical analysis may identify specific chart patterns or indicators suggesting bearish market trends, such as lower highs, lower lows, moving average crossovers, or breakdowns, signaling a potential decline in a stock's price.

Negative News or Catalysts: Any negative news related to a company, such as lawsuits, regulatory issues, product recalls, or executive misconduct, can create uncertainty and lead to a decline in investor confidence and stock price.

Macroeconomic Factors: Unfavorable macroeconomic indicators, such as high unemployment rates, economic recessions, inflation, or geopolitical tensions, can impact the overall stock market negatively and potentially result in a decline in stock prices across various sectors.

It's important to note that these warning signs do not guarantee a stock price decline, as the market is influenced by various factors and is **inherently** unpredictable. Thorough research, analysis, and diversification should always be considered before making investment decisions.

Determining stock value

The value of a stock is determined by various factors that can broadly be categorized into two approaches: fundamental analysis and market sentiment.

1. Fundamental analysis: This approach evaluates a stock's value based on the underlying financial performance, industry trends, and economic indicators. Key factors considered in fundamental analysis include:

> **Earnings and revenue:** Analysts assess a company's past and projected earnings growth, revenue trends, and profitability ratios to evaluate its financial health and potential for future growth.

> **Balance sheet and financial ratios:** Evaluating a company's assets, liabilities, and equity helps determine its financial stability. Key ratios like price-to-earnings (P/E), price-to-sales (P/S), and price-to-book (P/B) ratios provide insights into a stock's relative value compared to its earnings, revenues, and book value.

Management and competitive advantage: Assessing the company's management team, its strategic initiatives, and competitive advantages relative to its industry peers helps investors gauge its long-term prospects.

Industry and market dynamics: Understanding the industry dynamics, market trends, and competitive landscape can influence the valuation of a stock. Factors such as barriers to entry, innovation, and market demand for a company's products or services are considered.

Macroeconomic factors: The overall economic health, interest rates, inflation, and geopolitical factors can impact stock values across the market. Market cycles and economic indicators influence investor sentiment towards stocks.

2. Market sentiment: Stock prices are also influenced by investor sentiment, which can be driven by factors like:

News and public perception: Positive or negative news regarding a company, industry, or the overall market can impact investor sentiment. Changes in public perception, sentiment, or market rumors can lead to buying or selling pressure on a stock.

Investor expectations: Investor expectations of future performance, growth prospects, and market demand can drive stock prices. Positive sentiment and high expectations can push a stock's price above its intrinsic value, while pessimism can result in undervaluation.

Supply and demand: The basic principle of supply and demand affects stock prices. If there is high demand for a stock and limited supply, its price tends to rise. Conversely, if there is excess supply and lower demand, the price may decrease.

Technical analysis: Investors also use technical analysis to study past price trends, trading volumes, and chart patterns. Technical indicators and trading algorithms inform some investors' buying and selling decisions, impacting stock prices.

Fundamental Analysis Ratios Explained

There are several commonly used ratios in fundamental analysis that can help investors determine the value of a stock relative to its earnings, revenues, book value, and other financial metrics. These ratios provide insights into a stock's valuation and help investors make informed investment decisions. Here are a few of the most widely used ratios:

Price-to-Earnings Ratio (P/E): The P/E ratio compares the current market price of a stock to its earnings per share (EPS). It is calculated by dividing the stock price by the EPS. This ratio indicates how much investors are willing to pay for each dollar of the company's earnings. A higher P/E ratio suggests a higher valuation, indicating that investors expect higher future earnings growth. However, a high P/E ratio can also indicate an overvalued stock.

Price-to-Sales Ratio (P/S): The P/S ratio compares the market price of a stock to its revenue per share. It is calculated by dividing the stock price by the revenue per share. This ratio helps evaluate a company's valuation relative to its sales performance and can be particularly useful when a company has negative earnings or when comparing companies in industries where earnings are less relevant. A lower P/S ratio may indicate that a stock is undervalued, but it should be used in conjunction with other ratios for a comprehensive analysis.

Price-to-Book Ratio (P/B): The P/B ratio compares the market price of a stock to its book value per share. The book value represents the net worth of the company, calculated by subtracting liabilities from assets. The P/B ratio is calculated by dividing the stock price by the book value per share. This ratio provides insights into whether a stock is trading at a premium or discount to its book value. A low P/B ratio may indicate an undervalued stock, but it is important to consider industry norms and the company's specific circumstances.

Dividend Yield: The dividend yield is the ratio of the annual dividend payment per share to the stock price. It indicates the return an investor can expect in the form of dividends from holding the stock. Dividend yield is widely used by income-oriented investors who seek regular income from their investments. A higher dividend yield may suggest an attractive investment, but it is important to consider the company's dividend sustainability and growth prospects.

These ratios are just a few examples of the many financial metrics used to determine stock prices. It's important to analyze and interpret these ratios in the context of the company's industry, growth prospects, and overall market conditions.

Additionally, using multiple ratios and considering qualitative factors provides a more comprehensive view of a stock's value.

It's important to note that stock prices can be influenced by a combination of these factors and may fluctuate based on market conditions, news events, and investor behavior. Stock value is ultimately determined by the consensus of buyers and sellers in the market.

Stock Ticker

A stock ticker symbol, also known simply as a ticker symbol or a ticker, is a unique series of letters representing a particular company's publicly traded stock on a stock exchange. These symbols are used for quick and easy identification and tracking of stocks in financial markets and are widely used by investors, traders, and financial professionals.

Ticker symbols are typically short abbreviations, usually consisting of between one to five letters, that represent a specific company's stock. Companies listed on different stock exchanges may have different ticker symbols.

For instance, the ticker symbol for Apple Inc. is "AAPL" on the Nasdaq Stock Market, while it is "APPL" on the Frankfurt Stock Exchange. Ticker symbols are case-insensitive, meaning they can be entered in uppercase or lowercase letters interchangeably.

When checking stock prices or trading, individuals can search for a stock using its ticker symbol. It provides a quick and unambiguous way to identify and trade stocks as well as track their performance on various financial platforms and news outlets.

Chapter 5: Stock Charts And Technical Analysis

"Investing is not about being right or wrong; it's about how much money you make when you're right and how much you lose when you're wrong."
– George Soros

What Are Stock Charts

Stock charts are graphical representations of the historical price and volume data of a particular stock or a stock market index over a specified time period. They provide a visual tool for investors and traders to analyze market trends, identify patterns, and make informed decisions about buying or selling stocks. Here are some key components and types of stock charts:

Time on the x-axis: Stock charts typically display time on the horizontal or x-axis. This axis represents the time period for which the price and volume data are being plotted. It can span from minutes to years, depending on the desired level of detail.

Price on the y-axis: The vertical or y-axis of a stock chart represents the price of the stock or index being analyzed. Prices are plotted along this axis, allowing users to see the price movements over time.

Line chart: The simplest type of stock chart is the line chart, which connects the closing prices of a stock or index over time. It provides a basic visual representation of the stock's price trend.

Bar chart: A bar chart presents more information by displaying the high, low, opening, and closing prices of a stock or index for each time period. Each bar on the chart represents a specific period, such as a day, week, or month. The vertical lines of the bar indicate the high and low prices, while horizontal lines extending from the bar indicate the opening and closing prices.

Candlestick chart: Candlestick charts display the same information as bar charts but offer a more visually appealing representation. Each candlestick represents a specific time period and displays the opening, closing, high, and low prices. A filled or colored body indicates that the closing price was lower than the opening price, while an unfilled or hollow body signifies the closing price was higher than the opening price. Candlestick patterns are often used to identify market trends and reversals.

Volume: Many stock charts also include a volume chart or histogram, which shows the trading volume of the stock or index for each time period. Volume provides an indication of market activity and can help validate price movements.

Technical indicators: Stock charts often allow users to overlay various technical indicators, such as moving averages, **MACD (Moving Average Convergence Divergence)**, RSI (Relative Strength Index), or **Bollinger Bands**. These indicators provide additional insights into price trends, momentum, and potential market reversals.

Candlestick Charts Explained

Candlestick charts are a type of price chart used in technical analysis to display the open, high, low, and closing prices of a stock or security over a specific period of time. Each candlestick represents a specific time frame, such as a day, week, or hour, and provides valuable information about the price action during that period.

A candlestick chart is considered bullish or bearish based on the relationship between the opening and closing prices, as well as the overall shape of the candlestick. Here's how you can determine whether a candlestick is bullish or bearish:

1. Bullish Candlestick:
   - The closing price is higher than the opening price.
   - The body of the candlestick is usually colored or filled, typically in green or white (depending on the charting platform), to indicate strength or positive sentiment.
   - The upper shadow or wick (if present) represents the session's high price, while the lower shadow represents the session's low price, indicating that buyers were able to push prices higher.

2. Bearish Candlestick:
   - The opening price is higher than the closing price.
   - The body of the candlestick is usually hollow or colored, usually in red or black, to indicate weakness or negative sentiment.
   - The upper shadow or wick (if present) represents the session's high price, while the lower shadow represents the session's low price, indicating that sellers were able to push prices lower.

It's important to note that the length of the body and shadows relative to each other can provide additional information about the strength or weakness of the bullish or bearish sentiment. For example, a long bullish candlestick with little to no upper shadow suggests strong buying pressure, while a long bearish candlestick with little to no lower shadow suggests strong selling pressure. Traders often interpret the size and shape of candlesticks in combination with other technical analysis tools to make more accurate predictions about future price movements.

By analyzing stock charts, investors and traders can gain insights into historical price patterns, support and resistance levels, trend reversals, and market sentiment. This information can aid in making informed decisions about buying, selling, or holding stocks. However, it's important to note that stock charts should be used in conjunction with other fundamental and technical analysis tools to make well-rounded investment decisions.

Common Candlestick Patterns

A candlestick consists of a rectangular body and two thin lines, called shadows or wicks, extending from the top and bottom of the body. The body represents the range between the opening and closing prices, while the wicks represent the high and low prices during that time frame.

There are different types of candlestick patterns, each with its own interpretation and significance. Here are some common candlestick patterns:

Bullish/Bearish Engulfing: A bullish engulfing pattern occurs when a smaller bearish candlestick is followed by a larger bullish candlestick that engulfs the previous bearish candlestick, indicating a potential trend reversal. The opposite is true for a bearish engulfing pattern.

Doji: A doji candlestick has a small or nonexistent body, indicating that the opening and closing prices are very close or equal. It suggests indecision in the market and can be a potential sign of a trend reversal.

Hammer: A hammer candlestick has a small body and a long lower shadow, resembling a hammer. It suggests potential bullishness after a **downtrend** and indicates that buyers are stepping in to push prices higher.

Shooting Star: A shooting star candlestick has a small body and a long upper shadow, resembling an inverted hammer. It suggests potential bearishness after an **uptrend** and indicates that sellers may be taking control.

Morning Star/Evening Star: These are three-candlestick patterns. A morning star occurs during a downtrend and consists of a long bearish candlestick, followed by a smaller-bodied candlestick that gaps lower, and finally a long bullish candlestick. It suggests a potential trend reversal. An evening star is the opposite and occurs during an uptrend.

These are just a few examples of candlestick patterns, and there are many more that traders analyze to make decisions about buying or selling stocks. By observing patterns and combinations of candlesticks, traders can gain insights into market sentiment, identify potential trend reversals, and make more informed trading decisions.

What Is Technical Analysis

Technical analysis is a method of evaluating and predicting future price movements in stocks by examining past market data, primarily through the use of charts and other analytical tools. It focuses on the study of price patterns, trends, support and resistance levels, trading volume, and other indicators to identify potential buying or selling opportunities.

Technical analysts believe that historical price data holds valuable information that can help them predict future price movements. They assume that stock prices follow repeating patterns and trends and that these patterns can be used to forecast future price movements. Technical analysis can be used for short-term trading strategies, such as day trading or swing trading, as well as for longer-term investment decisions.

Some common tools and techniques used in technical analysis include trendlines, moving averages, chart patterns (such as triangles, head and shoulders, and double tops/bottoms), oscillators (such as the Relative Strength Index and Stochastic Oscillator), and support/resistance levels.

It is important to note that technical analysis is based on the historical price data and does not consider fundamental factors, such as a company's financials or industry trends. Therefore, it is often used in conjunction with fundamental analysis to make well-informed investment decisions.

Technical Indicators

Technical indicators are mathematical calculations applied to stock charts to provide insights into market trends, momentum, and potential reversals. They are used by investors and traders to make informed decisions about buying or selling stocks. Here are some common technical indicators used on stock charts:

> **Moving Averages (MA):** Moving averages are trend-following indicators that smooth out price fluctuations by calculating the average price over a specified period.

They help identify the direction and strength of a trend. Common types of moving averages include the Simple Moving Average (SMA) and the Exponential Moving Average (EMA).

Relative Strength Index (RSI): RSI is a momentum oscillator that gauges the speed and change of price movements. It oscillates between 0 and 100, with values above 70 indicating overbought conditions and values below 30 indicating oversold conditions. RSI can help identify potential trend reversals and divergences between price and momentum.

Moving Average Convergence Divergence (MACD): MACD is a trend-following momentum indicator that consists of two lines: the MACD line and the signal line. The MACD line is calculated by subtracting the 26-day EMA from the 12-day EMA. The signal line is a 9-day EMA of the MACD line. MACD crossovers and divergences can signal changes in trend direction and momentum.

Bollinger Bands: Bollinger Bands consist of three lines plotted on a price chart: the middle band (usually a 20-day moving average), the upper band (two standard deviations above the middle band), and the lower band (two standard deviations below the middle band). Bollinger Bands help identify periods of high or low volatility and can indicate potential price reversals.

Stochastic Oscillator: The Stochastic Oscillator is a momentum indicator that compares a stock's closing price to its price range over a specified period. It oscillates between 0 and 100, with values above 80 indicating overbought conditions and values below 20 indicating oversold conditions. The Stochastic Oscillator can help identify potential trend reversals and overbought/oversold levels.

Volume: Although volume is not a strictly technical indicator, it is often shown on stock charts as a histogram or line graph. Volume reflects the number of shares or contracts traded during a given period. Increased volume can confirm the strength of a price move or signal the beginning of a new trend.

These are just a few examples of the numerous technical indicators available. Traders and investors often use a combination of indicators to gain multiple perspectives on price movements and to confirm signals. It's important to understand the limitations and strengths of each indicator and to use them in conjunction with other technical analysis tools and fundamental analysis for comprehensive decision-making.

Chapter 6: How To Pick Winning Stocks

"Only buy something that you'd be perfectly happy to hold if the market shut down for 10 years." – Warren Buffett

Strategies To Pick Winning Stocks

Picking winning stocks to trade is a challenging task that requires careful analysis and research. While no strategy guarantees success, here are some commonly used approaches and factors to consider when selecting stocks:

Fundamental Analysis: This approach focuses on analyzing a company's financial health, including its earnings, revenue growth, profitability ratios, debt levels, and competitive position. Investors may review financial statements, SEC filings, company news, and industry trends to evaluate the stock's potential.

Technical Analysis: This strategy involves studying historical price patterns, trends, and trading volumes to identify potential entry and exit points. Technical analysts use charts, indicators, and patterns to analyze stock price movements, aiming to predict future price behavior based on past patterns.

Research and Due Diligence: Conduct thorough research on the company, its industry, competitors, and market trends. Look for catalysts that could impact the stock's performance, such as product launches, regulatory changes, or industry developments. Evaluate the company's management team, corporate governance practices, and reputation.

Valuation Metrics: Consider valuation metrics like price-to-earnings ratio (P/E), price-to-sales ratio (P/S), price-to-book ratio (P/B), and dividend yield. Compare these metrics to historical averages, peers in the industry, and the broader market to gauge if the stock is undervalued or overvalued.

Diversification: Diversify your portfolio by investing in different sectors or asset classes. This helps reduce risk by not putting all your eggs in one basket. Diversification allows for exposure to a variety of companies and industries, increasing the potential for overall portfolio stability.

Consider Risk-Reward Ratio: Evaluate the potential risks and rewards of the investment. Assess the stock's volatility, liquidity, and market conditions. Understand the potential downside risks and upside potential before making investment decisions.

Stay Informed: Continually track the company's news, market trends, and any material information that could impact the stock's performance. Regularly review quarterly reports, earnings releases, and conference calls.

It is worth mentioning that successful stock trading requires ongoing monitoring, adaptability, and a long-term perspective. It is advisable to consult with a financial advisor or engage in educational resources to enhance your understanding of investment strategies and risk management techniques.

Analyze Candlestick Charts To Find Stocks

Analyzing candlestick charts can provide valuable insights into the price movements and potential trends of a stock. Here are some basic steps to analyze candlestick charts and make informed decisions:

Familiarize yourself with Candlestick Patterns: Learn about different candlestick patterns and their significance. Common patterns include doji, hammer, engulfing, and shooting star. Each pattern signifies specific market sentiment and potential trend reversals.

Observe the Overall Trend: Identify the overall trend in the stock's price by assessing the sequence of candlesticks. An upward trend consists of higher highs and higher lows, while a downward trend features lower highs and lower lows. Understanding the trend can help you make better trading decisions.

Look for Reversal Patterns: Focus on candlestick patterns indicating potential trend reversals. For example, a hammer or a doji after a downtrend might suggest a reversal to an upward trend. Conversely, an engulfing pattern after an uptrend could signal a potential reversal to a downward trend.

Analyze Support and Resistance Levels: Identify key support and resistance levels on the chart. These levels indicate areas where the stock's price has historically encountered buying or selling pressure. A breakout or bounce off these levels can provide trading opportunities.

Consider Volume: Pay attention to the volume associated with different candlestick patterns. High volume during a specific candlestick can validate the significance of the pattern and indicate increased market participation.

Combine with Other Technical Indicators: Utilize other technical indicators, such as moving averages, relative strength index (RSI), or MACD, to confirm the signals provided by the candlestick patterns. This helps to strengthen your analysis and reduce false signals.

Validate with Fundamental Analysis: Combine your technical analysis with fundamental analysis to ensure a comprehensive evaluation. Consider factors like company financials, industry trends, news releases, and market sentiment. Fundamental analysis helps provide a broader context for your trading decisions.

Practice Risk Management: Implement proper risk management strategies, such as setting stop-loss orders or using position sizing, to protect your investments. Not every trade will be a winner, so it's crucial to limit potential losses and protect your capital.

Remember, while candlestick chart analysis can provide valuable insights, it should be part of a holistic approach to stock analysis. Consider utilizing other tools and seeking advice from professionals or experienced traders to enhance your decision-making process.

Search For Breakouts

Breakouts refer to price movements in which a stock, currency, or other financial instrument moves above a resistance level or below a support level, often with increased volume and momentum. Breakouts represent a significant shift in market sentiment and can provide trading opportunities for traders and investors.

Candlestick formations are a popular tool used by technical analysts to identify potential breakouts. Here are a few candlestick formations that can signal breakouts:

1. Bullish Breakout Signals:
  a. Bullish Engulfing Pattern: This occurs when a bullish candle "engulfs" the previous bearish candle, indicating potential buying pressure and a bullish breakout.

b. ***Morning Star****:* This formation consists of three candles - a bearish candle, a small indecisive candle, and a bullish candle - signaling a potential reversal and bullish breakout.

c. ***Three White Soldiers****:* This formation consists of three consecutive bullish candles with higher closes, suggesting strong buying pressure and a potential bullish breakout.

2. Bearish Breakout Signals:

a. ***Bearish Engulfing Pattern:*** This occurs when a bearish candle "engulfs" the previous bullish candle, indicating potential selling pressure and a bearish breakout.

b. ***Evening Star:*** This formation is the opposite of the Morning Star, consisting of three candles - a bullish candle, a small indecisive candle, and a bearish candle - signaling a potential reversal and bearish breakout.

c. ***Three Black Crows:*** This formation consists of three consecutive bearish candles with lower closes, suggesting strong selling pressure and a potential bearish breakout.

It's important to note that candlestick formations alone cannot guarantee successful breakouts. Traders should consider other factors like **volume**, trend lines, support and resistance levels to validate breakouts and make trading decisions. We will go in depth about trend lines, support and resistance levels in chapter 10.

How To Use Volume To Find Stocks

Volume is an important indicator that can help in finding stocks with potential trading opportunities. Here's a general approach on how to use volume to find stocks:

Look for unusual volume: Start by identifying stocks with unusually high trading volume compared to their average daily volume. A significant increase in trading volume can indicate increased interest, buying or selling pressure, and potentially signify market-moving news or events related to the stock.

Analyze volume patterns: Examine the volume patterns of stocks over time to identify trends or patterns. For example, increasing volume with rising stock prices might indicate bullish sentiment and upward momentum. On the other hand, high volume accompanied by declining prices might suggest bearish sentiment and selling pressure. By analyzing volume patterns, you can gain insights into market sentiment and potential future price movements.

Confirm price trends with volume: Volume can be used to validate or confirm price trends. If a stock is experiencing an upward or downward trend, high volume during the price movement reinforces the strength of the trend. If there is a divergence between price and volume, such as increasing prices with decreasing volume, it might indicate an upcoming reversal or weakening of the trend.

Compare volume to historical data: Compare the current volume of a stock to its historical trading volume. By analyzing how the current volume compares to past trading patterns, you can identify whether the current volume is above or below average, and if there is any significant deviation that might indicate a trading opportunity or potential market reaction.

Combine volume analysis with other indicators: Volume should not be analyzed in isolation but in conjunction with other technical indicators or fundamental analysis. For example, combining volume analysis with price oscillators, moving averages, or trend lines can provide a more comprehensive view of a stock's potential opportunities and risks.

Remember, volume analysis is just one tool among many used in technical analysis. It is important to consider other factors, such as company fundamentals, news events, and market trends, to make well-informed investment decisions.

Using stop-loss orders and proper risk management techniques is crucial when trading breakouts to protect against false breakouts or unexpected reversals.

Choose Dividend Stocks!

Dividends are a portion of a company's profits that are distributed to its shareholders as a form of payment. When a company generates profits, it can choose to reinvest them back into the business or distribute them to shareholders in the form of dividends.

Dividends are typically paid in cash, although some companies may offer dividends in the form of additional shares of stock or other assets. Dividends are usually paid on a regular basis, such as quarterly, semi-annually, or annually, depending on the company's policy.

Here are a few key points to understand about dividends:

Shareholder Benefit: Dividends are a way for companies to share their financial success with shareholders, providing them with a direct financial benefit.

Income Stream: Dividends can serve as a regular income stream for investors, especially for those who rely on investment income for living expenses.

Dividend Yield: The dividend yield is a percentage that represents the annual dividend payment relative to the stock price. It is often used by investors to compare dividend-paying stocks and evaluate the income potential of an investment.

Dividend Policies: Companies can have different dividend policies. Some companies have a consistent and predictable history of paying dividends, while others may not pay dividends at all. The decision to pay dividends is typically made by the company's board of directors.

Dividend Reinvestment Plans (DRIPs): Some companies offer dividend reinvestment plans, allowing shareholders to automatically reinvest their dividends to purchase additional shares of stock. This can help investors compound their investment over time.

It's important to note that not all companies pay dividends, especially young or growing companies that may choose to reinvest all profits back into the business for expansion and development. Before investing in a stock for its dividend, it's crucial to

research the company's dividend history, financial
health, and overall investment prospects.

Chapter 7: Entering and Exiting Trades

"The stock market is like a casino with the odds in your favor. If you play long enough, you are almost certain to win." – Peter Lynch

Placing Orders With Your Brokerage

There are several different types of brokerage orders that investors can use to place their buy or sell orders for **securities**. The most common types of brokerage orders include:

Market Order: A market order is the most straightforward type of order, where the investor instructs the broker to execute the trade immediately at the current market price. The trade is typically executed as soon as possible, and the investor may not have control over the exact price at which the order is filled. Market orders guarantee execution but not the price.

Limit Order: A limit order allows the investor to specify the maximum price (for a sell order) or minimum price (for a buy order) at which they are willing to execute the trade. The order will be filled only if the market reaches or crosses the specified limit price. Limit orders provide control over the execution price but do not guarantee the execution of the trade.

Stop Order (Stop-Loss Order): A stop order is an order that becomes a market order once a specified price (the stop price) is reached. A stop-loss order is a type of stop order used to limit potential losses. For example, a sell stop order can be placed below the current market price, and if the market reaches or falls below the stop price, the order will be executed as a market order. Stop orders are commonly used for managing risk and protecting gains.

Stop-Limit Order: A stop-limit order combines elements of both a stop order and a limit order. It becomes a limit order to buy or sell a security once a specified stop price is reached or breached. However, the order will only be executed within the specified price limit or better. This type of order offers more control over the execution price than a regular stop order but may not guarantee execution if the specified price limit is not reached.

Trailing Stop Order: A trailing stop order is a dynamic order that adjusts the stop price as the market price moves. For a trailing stop sell order, the stop price is set below the current market price by a certain percentage or amount. If the market price increases, the stop price follows and remains a certain fixed amount or percentage below the highest price since the order was placed. It is often used to lock in profits while allowing for potential further upside.

These are some of the common types of brokerage orders. Understanding the different order types and their implications is crucial for managing investments effectively and aligning trading strategies with specific investment goals and risk tolerance. It is recommended to familiarize oneself with the specific trading platform or broker's order types and rules, as they may vary slightly.

Entering and Exiting Strategies and Criteria

Entering and exiting trades refers to the process of buying or selling securities in the financial markets. Here are the steps typically involved in entering and exiting a trade:

Entering a Trade:

Research and Analysis: Before entering a trade, conduct thorough research and analysis to identify potential investment opportunities. Analyze factors such as company fundamentals, market trends, and technical indicators to make informed decisions.

Determine Trading Strategy: Define your trading strategy, including factors such as the type of securities you want to trade, the desired entry price, and the position size you are comfortable with. This will help guide your decision-making process.

Place Trade Orders: Use a brokerage account or trading platform to place your trade orders. Depending on your strategy, you can use different types of orders, such as market orders (buying or selling at the current market price) or limit orders (buying or selling at a specific price or better).

Monitor Execution: After placing your trade orders, monitor the execution to ensure they are filled correctly. Review any transaction costs, such as commissions or fees, associated with the trade.

The specific criteria for entering a trade will vary depending on individual trading strategies, risk tolerance, and market conditions. However, here are some common criteria considered by traders when entering and exiting a trade:

Entering a Trade:

Technical Analysis: Technical analysis involves using various chart patterns, indicators, and price action to make trading decisions. Traders may look for signals such as trend reversals, breakouts, support and resistance levels, moving averages, or other technical patterns that suggest a favorable entry point.

Fundamental Analysis: Fundamental analysis focuses on assessing the intrinsic value of a security by analyzing factors such as company financials, industry trends, management performance, and macroeconomic conditions. Traders may use fundamental analysis to identify undervalued or overvalued assets and make trading decisions based on their assessment.

Confirmation of Signals: Traders often seek confirmation of their analysis from multiple sources or indicators. This can involve cross-verifying signals from different technical indicators or aligning technical signals with positive fundamental developments or news.

Risk-Reward Ratio: Traders consider the potential risk-reward ratio before entering a trade. This involves assessing the potential profit target relative to the potential loss (or stop loss level) to determine if the potential reward justifies the risk taken. A favorable risk-reward ratio is often preferred to ensure the potential for profit outweighs the potential loss.

Volume and Liquidity: Volume and liquidity are essential considerations for traders. Higher trading volumes and liquidity indicate increased market efficiency and reduce the risk of trading at unfavorable prices. Traders may look for increased trading activity and liquidity when considering entering a trade.

Timing and Entry Signals: Traders may employ various techniques to determine optimal entry timing, such as using momentum indicators, oscillators, or price action signals. The aim is to enter a trade when the market conditions align with the trading strategy, suggesting a higher probability of success.

Risk Management: Proper risk management is crucial when entering a trade. Traders consider their risk tolerance and set parameters for position sizing, stop loss levels, and position diversification to protect their capital and manage potential losses.

It's important to note that these criteria are not exhaustive, and traders may utilize a combination of factors or develop their own unique strategies. Each trader's approach may differ based on their individual preferences, knowledge, and experience.

Exiting a Trade:

Define Exit Criteria: Determine your exit criteria before entering a trade. This can be based on your profit target, risk tolerance, or specific technical or fundamental indicators that signal an exit opportunity. Having predefined exit criteria helps avoid emotion-driven decision making.

Set Stop Loss and Take Profit Levels: Consider setting stop loss and take profit levels to manage potential risks and rewards. A stop loss order automatically sells or buys a security when it reaches a specified price to limit potential losses. A take profit order automatically closes a position when it reaches a certain profit level.

Monitor Trade Performance: Continuously monitor the performance of your trade. Keep an eye on factors like market conditions, news, and indicators that may influence the outcome of your trade.

Exit the Trade: Once your predefined exit criteria are met, execute the trade exit. You can manually close the position through your brokerage account or set a stop loss or take profit order to automatically trigger the exit.

The criteria for exiting a trade will depend on the individual's trading strategy, goals, and risk tolerance. Here are some common criteria considered by traders when determining the appropriate time to exit a trade:

Profit Target: Traders may set a specific profit target based on their strategy, risk-reward ratio, or technical indicators. Once the trade reaches the desired profit level, they may choose to exit the trade to secure the gains.

Stop Loss: Setting a stop loss is a risk management technique where traders establish a predetermined price level at which they will automatically exit the trade to limit potential losses. Stop loss orders are typically placed below the entry price for long positions and above the entry price for short positions.

Trailing Stop Loss: Some traders use a trailing stop loss, which is a dynamic approach to exit a trade. With a trailing stop loss, the stop loss level is adjusted as the trade moves in the trader's favor. This allows the trader to lock in profits as the price increases while still providing some flexibility for further upside potential.

Technical Indicators: Traders may use technical indicators to generate exit signals. For example, a trader who entered a trade based on a specific indicator may choose to exit when the indicator shows a reversal or a signal to close the position.

Reaching a Specific Price Level or Target: Traders may have specific price levels or targets in mind when entering a trade. Once the price reaches that level, they may decide to exit the trade, regardless of other factors.

Change in Market Conditions or News: If there is a significant change in market conditions, unexpected news, or events that could impact the position, traders may choose to exit the trade to minimize potential risk or take advantage of new opportunities.

Time-based Exit: Some traders may have a predefined time horizon for their trades. They may decide to exit the trade after a certain period, regardless of the profit or loss, to adhere to a specific trading plan or strategy.

Profit/loss ratio: Traders may consider the overall profit/loss ratio of their trades. If a series of trades shows consistently negative outcomes or fails to meet expected profit targets, they may choose to exit the trade to protect their capital or reevaluate their strategy.

It is important for traders to have a clear plan for exiting their trades and to stick to their predefined criteria. This helps ensure disciplined decision-making and effective risk management.

Chapter 8:Taxes

"The best investment you can make is in yourself."
– Warren Buffett

What Are Taxes?

Taxes are **mandatory** financial charges or levies imposed by the government on individuals, businesses, or other entities to fund public services and governmental operations. The government uses tax revenue to finance various sectors like healthcare, education, defense, infrastructure, social welfare programs, and more.

Brokerage accounts have both tax benefits and tax obligations that investors should be aware of. It's important to note that tax laws vary by **jurisdiction**, so it's recommended to consult with a tax professional or advisor for specific guidance. However, here are some general concepts related to the tax implications of brokerage accounts:

Tax Benefits:

> **Capital Gains Tax Deferral:** One of the significant tax benefits of a brokerage account is the ability to defer capital gains tax until the investment is sold. Unlike

retirement accounts (such as IRAs and 401(k)s), there is generally no tax penalty for withdrawing funds from a brokerage account before retirement age.

Step-up in Cost Basis: When an investor passes away, the cost basis of the assets held in the brokerage account is reset to their current market value. This means that heirs receive the assets with a stepped-up cost basis, potentially reducing the taxable capital gains if they decide to sell the assets.

Flexibility in Investment Strategy: Brokerage accounts offer flexibility in terms of investment options and strategies. Investors can choose from a wide range of securities like stocks, bonds, ETFs, mutual funds, and more, allowing for greater control and diversification in their investment portfolio.

Tax Obligations:

Capital Gains Tax: When an investor sells a security held in a brokerage account at a profit, they are liable to pay capital gains tax on the difference between the purchase price (cost basis) and the selling price. The tax rate depends on the investor's income and how long the securities were held (short-term vs. long-term capital gains).

Dividend and Interest Income: Any dividends or interest earned from investments held in a brokerage account are considered taxable income in the year they are received.

Required Reporting: Investors are obligated to report their earnings and pay applicable taxes on their brokerage account transactions. This may include providing accurate cost basis information for sold securities.

Wash Sale Rules: The IRS has wash sale rules that limit the ability to claim capital losses when buying substantially identical securities within 30 days of selling at a loss. This rule is designed to prevent investors from engaging in tax-motivated trading strategies.

It's crucial to keep accurate records of all transactions within a brokerage account to ensure compliance with tax obligations and to help calculate capital gains or losses correctly. Given the complexity of tax regulations, it's advisable to consult with a tax professional or advisor who can provide personalized tax advice based on individual circumstances and local tax laws.

Chapter 9: Managing Emotions

"The four most dangerous words in investing are: 'This time it's different.'" – Sir John Templeton

Manage Your Emotions

Managing emotions while trading is crucial for successful and rational decision-making. Here's why it's important:

Avoiding Impulsive Decisions: Emotions such as fear, greed, and excitement can cloud judgment and lead to impulsive trading decisions. Emotional trading often results in buying or selling stocks based on short-term fluctuations or market noise, rather than a well-thought-out strategy. By managing emotions, traders can avoid impulsive actions and make decisions based on rational analysis and long-term goals.

Sticking to a Trading Plan: Creating and following a trading plan is essential for consistent success. Emotions can tempt traders to deviate from their plan, leading to inconsistency and potentially poor outcomes. When emotions are well-managed, traders are more likely to adhere to their predetermined strategies, maintain discipline, and execute trades based on thorough analysis.

Minimizing Emotional Stress: Trading can be stressful, especially during periods of market volatility or unexpected events. Emotions like fear and anxiety can amplify stress levels, leading to emotional exhaustion or burnout. By managing emotions, traders can reduce stress and maintain a healthier mental state, enabling them to make objective decisions and perform more effectively in trading activities.

Avoiding Overtrading: Emotional trading can lead to excessive trading activity, also known as overtrading. This may occur when traders chase quick profits, act on impulses, or attempt to recover losses hastily. Overtrading increases transaction costs, exposes traders to unnecessary risks, and can negatively impact overall portfolio performance. By managing emotions and maintaining discipline, traders can avoid overtrading and focus on high-quality opportunities.

Mitigating Loss Aversion Bias: Loss aversion bias is a cognitive bias where individuals experience the pain of losses more strongly than the pleasure of gains. This bias can lead traders to hold onto losing positions for too long, refusing to cut their losses and hoping for a reversal. By managing emotions and objectively assessing trades, traders can mitigate loss aversion bias and make timely decisions to protect their capital.

Improving Emotional Resilience: The financial markets can be unpredictable, and losses are inevitable at times. Managing emotions helps traders develop emotional resilience, allowing them to bounce back from setbacks, learn from mistakes, and maintain a long-term perspective. Emotional resilience helps traders stay focused, make calculated decisions, and persist in their trading strategies over time.

What is FOMO?

FOMO, short for "Fear of Missing Out," is a common emotion experienced by investors in relation to stocks. It refers to the fear or anxiety that one might miss out on a potentially profitable investment opportunity or the fear of not being part of a particular market trend.

In the context of stocks, FOMO arises when investors observe others making significant gains or when they see a particular stock rapidly increasing in value. They fear that if they do not invest in that stock, they will miss out on potential profits or be left behind while others profit.

FOMO can influence investment decisions and lead to impulsive and irrational behavior. Investors may feel pressured to buy stocks without conducting proper research or analysis, solely driven by the fear of missing out on potential gains.

However, it is important to note that FOMO can be risky. Market trends can be volatile, and just because a stock is rising rapidly does not guarantee that it will continue to do so. Making investment decisions based solely on FOMO can lead to poor investment choices and potential losses.

It is crucial for investors to approach stock investments with a **rational** mindset, conduct thorough research, and consider their own investment goals and risk tolerance. Building a well-structured investment strategy based on careful analysis is typically more **prudent** than succumbing to the emotions driven by FOMO.

Overall, managing emotions while trading is essential for maintaining rationality, discipline, and consistency. By controlling emotions, traders can make more objective decisions, stick to their trading plans, reduce stress, avoid overtrading, mitigate biases, and develop emotional **resilience** for long-term success in the financial markets.

Chapter 10: All things Options

"In the midst of difficulty lies opportunity." - Albert Einstein

Options trading is a type of investment strategy that involves the buying and selling of options contracts, which are derivative financial instruments. Options represent the right, but not the obligation, to buy or sell an underlying asset at a predetermined price (known as the strike price) within a specific time frame (known as the expiration date).

Types Of Options Contracts

An options contract is a financial derivative that provides the holder with the right, but not the obligation, to buy or sell an underlying asset at a predetermined price within a specific time period. These contracts are typically traded on an options exchange and are standardized in terms of the underlying asset, contract size, expiration date, and strike price.

There are two types of options contracts: call options and put options.

1. Call Options: A call option gives the holder the right to buy an underlying asset at a specified price (known as the strike price) within a predetermined time frame. The holder of a call option expects the price of the underlying asset to increase before the expiration date. If this expectation is correct, the holder can exercise the option and buy the asset at a lower price than the current market price. However, if the asset price does not reach or exceed the strike price by the expiration date, the call option may expire worthless.

2. Put Options: A put option gives the holder the right to sell an underlying asset at a specified price (strike price) within a predetermined time frame. Holders of put options anticipate a decline in the price of the underlying asset. If the asset's price decreases below the strike price, the option holder can exercise the put option, selling the asset at a higher price than the prevailing market price. If the asset price remains above the strike price or fails to move significantly below it, the put option may expire worthless.

Options contracts are usually **standardized** and have **predetermined** expiration dates, typically falling on a specific day of the month. The expiration dates can range from a few days to several years. Investors can choose options contracts with different expiration periods depending on their investment objectives and time horizon.

Each options contract represents a specific quantity of the underlying asset, often referred to as the contract size or lot size. For stocks, one options contract often represents 100 shares of the underlying stock. Contract sizes can vary for different assets.

Options contracts also have a strike price, which is the predetermined price at which the holder can buy or sell the underlying asset. The strike price is fixed at the time the options contract is created and remains unchanged until the option expires.

It's important to note that options trading involves risks, including the potential loss of the premium paid for the option. Additionally, options contracts have limited lifespan and can expire worthless if the underlying asset's price does not move as anticipated. Understanding the characteristics of options contracts and analyzing market trends is crucial for successful options trading.

Determining An Options Contracts Value

The intrinsic value and extrinsic value are two components that determine the total value of an options contract.

> **Intrinsic value:** The intrinsic value of an options contract is the portion of its value that is determined by the underlying asset's

price relative to the strike price. For call options, the intrinsic value is the difference between the underlying asset's current price and the strike price, if it is higher than zero. For put options, the intrinsic value is the difference between the strike price and the underlying asset's current price, if it is higher than zero. Intrinsic value represents the immediate profit that can be obtained by exercising the option.

Extrinsic value (Time value): Extrinsic value, also known as time value, is the component of an options contract's value that is not related to the underlying asset's current price but to other factors such as time until expiration, volatility, interest rates, and market conditions. This value reflects the potential for the option to gain additional value over time. As an options contract gets closer to its expiration date, the extrinsic value tends to decrease.

Understanding the intrinsic and extrinsic value of options contracts is crucial for investors as it helps assess the overall value and potential profitability of the contract. Investors should consider both components when making decisions about buying, selling, or exercising options contracts.

Options Trading Strategies

Options trading offers several strategies, including buying or selling options contracts outright, as well as complex strategies involving combinations of options positions. Some common strategies include:

Call or Put Buying: Investors can buy call options if they expect the price of the underlying asset to rise, or put options if they anticipate a decline.

Covered Call: This strategy involves selling call options against stocks already owned. If the price of the stock remains below the strike price, the option will expire worthless, and the investor keeps the premium received from selling the option.

Protective Put: Investors can protect their stock positions by buying put options. If the stock price drops, the put option will increase in value and offset some of the losses.

Straddle and Strangle: These strategies involve buying both call and put options (straddle) or out-of-the-money call and put options (strangle) to profit from significant price volatility. The idea is to profit from a substantial move in either direction, regardless of whether it is up or down.

Long Straddle: A long straddle strategy involves buying both a call and a put option with the same strike price and expiration date. The strategy profits from significant price movements in either direction, regardless of the specific direction.

Iron Condor: This is a combination of two credit spreads, both a bear call spread and a bull put spread. It is a neutral strategy used when the investor expects a stock's price to remain within a certain range.

Butterfly Spread: Butterfly spread involves buying two options with a specific strike price and simultaneously selling two options with a strike price higher and lower than the bought options. It is a strategy used when the investor expects minimal price movement.

Calendar Spread: In this strategy, an investor buys an option with a longer-term expiration date and simultaneously sells an option with the same strike price but with a shorter-term expiration date. It aims to profit from time decay while minimizing price movement risk.

Strangle: A strangle strategy involves simultaneously buying out-of-the-money call and put options with the same expiration date. It profits from significant price movement but does not require the specific direction of the move.

Options trading allows investors to gain exposure to assets without directly owning them, providing flexibility and potential for profit. However, it's important to note that options trading is complex and carries risks, including the possibility of losing the entire investment. It requires understanding of the options market, underlying assets, and thorough analysis of market trends before participating in options trading activities.

Example Of Buying A Call Option

Let's say you are an investor who believes that the price of stock ABC, currently trading at $50 per share, will significantly increase over the next three months. Instead of buying the stock directly, you decide to purchase a call option contract without executing it. Here's how it could work:

1. You research and analyze the options market for stock ABC and identify a call option contract that aligns with your price target and timeframe. Let's assume you choose to purchase one ABC call option contract with a strike price of $55, expiring in three months, and a premium of $3 per contract.

2. As the buyer of the call option, you pay the premium upfront to the options exchange. In this

case, you would pay $300 ($3 x 100) for the one contract.

3. By purchasing this call option contract, you secure the right, but not the obligation, to buy 100 shares of ABC at the strike price of $55 per share, anytime before or at the expiration date.

4. The options contract gives you leverage, as you potentially stand to profit from the price increase of ABC's stock without tying up a significant amount of capital. If the price of ABC rises above the strike price of $55 during the lifetime of the contract, the value of the call option could increase, allowing you to sell it in the options market for a higher premium.

5. However, if the price of ABC does not reach or exceed the strike price of $55 before the expiration of the contract, the call option might expire worthless. In this scenario, you would lose the premium paid ($300) but would not be obligated to exercise the option.

It's important to note that buying call options without executing them can be a speculative strategy with significant risks. The value of options can fluctuate, influenced by various factors such as market volatility, time decay, and the underlying stock price. Traders should carefully consider their risk tolerance, investment objectives, and undertake thorough analysis before engaging in options trading. Seeking advice from a financial professional is always a prudent approach.

Exercising Options

Exercising an option refers to the act of utilizing the rights granted by an options contract. When an option holder decides to exercise their option, they are choosing to buy or sell the underlying asset at the predetermined strike price.

The decision to exercise an option depends on the type of option and the market conditions:

1. ***Call Option***: If an investor holds a call option and believes that the price of the underlying asset will increase, they can choose to exercise the option. By doing so, they can buy the underlying asset at the strike price, regardless of its current market price. This allows the option holder to profit from the difference between the strike price and the asset's higher market value.

2. ***Put Option:*** If an investor holds a put option and expects the price of the underlying asset to decline, they can exercise the option. By doing so, they can sell the underlying asset at the strike price, regardless of its lower market price. This enables the option holder to gain from the

difference between the strike price and the asset's lower market value.

It's important to note that exercising an option is not compulsory. The option holder has the right, but not the obligation, to exercise. They can choose to let the option expire without exercising it if it is not profitable to do so.

Factors such as the market price of the underlying asset and the remaining time until the option's expiration date influence the decision to exercise. If the option is out of the money (the asset price is not favorable for exercise) or the remaining time is limited, it may not be beneficial to exercise the option. In such cases, it is often more economical to sell the option on the market instead.

Exercising an options contract typically involves contacting the broker or the options exchange to initiate the necessary transactions. The specifics of the process can vary based on the exchange and the brokerage firm being used.

Understanding the rights and obligations associated with options contracts and carefully evaluating market conditions are crucial when deciding whether or not to exercise an option.

Let's consider an example involving a call option contract on shares of Apple Inc. (AAPL).

Suppose an investor holds a call option contract with a strike price of $150 and an expiration date of December 31, 2022. The current market price of Apple's stock is $160 per share.

If the investor believes that the price of Apple stock will continue to rise and exceed $150 by the expiration date, they may choose to exercise the option.

On December 31, 2022, Apple's stock price reached $180 per share. The option holder decides to exercise their call option and buy the shares at the predetermined $150 strike price.

By exercising the option, the investor has the right to purchase the shares at $150, even though the market price is higher. This allows the investor to gain an immediate profit of $30 per share ($180 market price - $150 strike price).

After exercising the call option, the investor becomes the owner of Apple shares and can either retain them in their portfolio or sell them at the prevailing market price, subject to any further trading restrictions or considerations.

It's essential to note that exercising options may also involve transaction costs and potential tax implications. It's advisable to consult with a financial professional or broker for specific guidance based on individual circumstances.

Explaining the Greeks

The Greeks in options trading are a set of mathematical measurements used to understand and quantify the various factors that can influence the price and risk characteristics of an options contract. They help traders and investors assess and manage their options positions more effectively. Let's look at some of the key Greek measures and their impact on option contract prices:

Delta: Delta measures the sensitivity of an option's price to changes in the price of the underlying asset. It ranges from -1 to +1 for put and call options, respectively. A higher delta indicates that the option price will move in tandem with the underlying asset. For example, a call option with a delta of 0.70 will increase in price by $0.70 for every $1 increase in the underlying stock price.

Gamma: Gamma measures the rate at which delta changes as the underlying asset's price changes. It represents the curvature of the options' delta. Gamma is particularly relevant for traders focused on dynamic hedging strategies to manage delta exposure. Higher gamma means delta will change more rapidly with small movements in the underlying asset's price.

Theta: Theta measures the effect of time decay on an option's price. It represents the rate at which the option's value decreases as time passes. Theta is usually negative for options, implying that the option's price will gradually erode over time, all else being equal. As expiration approaches, theta tends to accelerate, meaning options lose value more rapidly.

Vega: Vega measures an option's sensitivity to changes in implied volatility (the market's expectations for future price fluctuations). It quantifies the impact of volatility on an option's price. Higher vega indicates that options will be more affected by changes in implied volatility.

Rho: Rho measures an option's sensitivity to changes in interest rates. It estimates how the option's price may change as interest rates fluctuate. Rho is generally more relevant for longer-term options and can become more pronounced in scenarios where interest rate movements are significant.

These Greek measures are not fully independent but rather interrelated. Understanding their dynamics helps traders assess the risk and potential profitability of their option positions, manage portfolio exposure, and select suitable trading strategies. It's important to note that the Greeks are not fixed values and can change as market conditions evolve.

Credit and Debit Spreads

Credit and debit spreads are options trading strategies that involve simultaneously buying and selling multiple options contracts to create a spread position. The primary difference between the two lies in the initial cash flow of the strategy.

1. Credit Spreads: Credit spreads involve selling an option with a higher premium and simultaneously buying an option with a lower premium. As a result, the strategy generates a net credit to the trader's account. The premium received from selling the option is higher than the premium paid for buying the option, hence creating a credit.

> **Bullish Credit Spread:** This strategy is implemented when the trader expects the underlying asset's price to increase. It involves selling an out-of-the-money put option with a higher premium and simultaneously buying an even further out-of-the-money put option.

> **Bearish Credit Spread:** This strategy is implemented when the trader believes the

underlying asset's price will decrease. It involves selling an out-of-the-money call option with a higher premium and simultaneously buying an even further out-of-the-money call option.

In both cases, the credit received from selling one option offsets the cost of purchasing the other option, resulting in a net credit. The maximum profit is limited to the net credit received, while the maximum loss is limited to the width between the two strike prices minus the net credit.

2. Debit Spreads: Debit spreads involve buying an option with a higher premium and simultaneously selling an option with a lower premium. As a result, the strategy requires an initial cash outflow or debit from the trader's account.

Bullish Debit Spread: This strategy is implemented when the trader expects the underlying asset's price to increase. It involves buying an in-the-money call option with a higher premium and simultaneously selling an out-of-the-money call option with a lower premium.

Bearish Debit Spread: This strategy is implemented when the trader believes the underlying asset's price will decrease. It involves buying an in-the-money put option with a higher premium and simultaneously selling an out-of-the-money put option with a lower premium.

In both cases, the cost of buying the in-the-money option is partially offset by the premium received from selling the out-of-the-money option, resulting in a net debit. The maximum profit is limited to the difference between the two strike prices minus the net debit, while the maximum loss is limited to the net debit paid.

Both credit and debit spreads have their own risk/reward profiles and are used in different market situations. Traders should assess their views on the underlying asset, their risk tolerance, and the potential profit/loss scenarios before implementing either strategy.

Let's consider an example of executing a debit spread trade using options on stock XYZ:

1. Stock XYZ is currently trading at $50 per share, and you have a bullish outlook on the stock's price in the near term.

2. You decide to implement a debit spread strategy using call options.

   - **Step 1**: Buy an in-the-money call option: You buy one XYZ call option with a strike price of $45 expiring in one month. This option has a premium of $6 per contract, and since each contract represents 100 shares, the total cost is $600 ($6 x 100).

- **Step 2**: Sell an out-of-the-money call option: You simultaneously sell one XYZ call option with a strike price of $55 expiring in one month. This option has a premium of $2 per contract, so you receive a credit of $200 ($2 x 100).

- Overall, the net debit for executing this debit spread trade is $400 ($600 - $200).

3. Potential outcomes:

- If at expiration the stock price is below the sold call option's strike price of $55, both options expire worthless, and you lose the net debit of $400.

- If at expiration the stock price is above the bought call option's strike price of $45, but below the sold call option's strike price of $55, the bought call option would have intrinsic value, while the sold call option expires worthless. You can exercise the bought call option and sell the underlying shares at the higher price, benefiting from the price increase and potentially offsetting part or all of the initial debit.

- If at expiration the stock price is above the sold call option's strike price of $55, both options would have intrinsic value. In this case, you may choose to exercise the bought option and sell the shares at the higher price, while the sold option would be exercised against you. The maximum potential profit is the difference between the two strike prices ($55 - $45 = $10) minus the net debit ($10 - $4 = $6) or $600.

Charting For Options Trades

Charting on a stock candlestick chart is a popular technique used by traders and investors to determine the direction of a stock's price movement. Candlestick charts provide a visual representation of the stock's trading activity over a specific period. Here's an explanation of how to interpret a candlestick chart to analyze stock direction:

1. Candlestick Basics:
   - Each candlestick on the chart represents a specific time period, such as a day, week, or hour.
   - The body of the candlestick illustrates the price range between the stock's opening and closing prices for that period.
   - The upper and lower shadows, also known as wicks or tails, show the high and low prices reached during that period.

2. Bullish and Bearish Candlesticks:
   - *Bullish candlesticks:* When the closing price is higher than the opening price, the candlestick is usually colored white, green, or any other color

representing a bullish sentiment. The upper shadow indicates the high price, and the lower shadow represents the low price.

- ***Bearish candlesticks:*** When the closing price is lower than the opening price, the candlestick is usually colored black, red, or any other color representing a bearish sentiment. The upper shadow denotes the high price, and the lower shadow represents the low price.

3. Patterns and Trends:

- By observing multiple candlesticks over time, chartists look for patterns and trends that suggest potential price movements.

- ***Bullish patterns:*** Patterns such as "hammer," "bullish engulfing," and "morning star" indicate potential reversals or uptrends.

- ***Bearish patterns:*** Patterns like "shooting star," "bearish engulfing," and "evening star" suggest potential reversals or downtrends.

4. Support and Resistance Levels:

- Chartists identify key support and resistance levels based on previous price action and candlestick patterns.

- ***Support level:*** When the stock's price falls to a certain point repeatedly but fails to go lower, it indicates a level where buying pressure may increase, potentially leading to a price rebound.

- ***Resistance level:*** When the stock's price reaches a certain point repeatedly but fails to exceed it, it indicates a level where selling pressure may increase, potentially causing the price to drop.

5. Moving Averages and Indicators:
   - Adding moving averages and technical indicators to candlestick charts can provide further insight.
   - Moving averages smooth out price data and help identify trend direction.
   - Oscillators such as the Relative Strength Index (RSI) or Moving Average Convergence Divergence (MACD) can help determine overbought or oversold conditions.

By combining these elements, traders and investors can analyze candlestick charts to identify potential stock directions and make more informed decisions when buying options contracts. However, candlestick charting is just one tool and should be used alongside other forms of analysis and risk management strategies.

Charting Trend Lines For Options Trades

Charting trend lines on stock charts is a technique widely used by traders and investors to identify and analyze trends in stock prices. These trend lines help to visualize the overall direction of the stock's price movement and can provide valuable insights for making trading decisions. Here's an explanation of how to draw and interpret trend lines on stock charts:

1. Identifying a Trend:
- Before drawing a trend line, it's crucial to determine the direction of the trend – whether it is an uptrend, downtrend, or sideways trend.
- An uptrend is characterized by a series of higher highs and higher lows, indicating a stock's price is generally moving upward.
- A downtrend is characterized by a series of lower highs and lower lows, indicating a stock's price is generally moving downward.
- A sideways trend, also known as a range-bound market, occurs when the stock's price moves within a relatively horizontal range.

2. Drawing an Uptrend Line:
- To draw an uptrend line, connect the series of higher lows using a straight line. The line should be drawn below the price bars.
- Once at least two higher lows are connected, extending the line to the right can help identify potential support levels in the future.
- The more times the price touches or bounces off the uptrend line without breaking it, the more significant the trend line becomes.

3. Drawing a Downtrend Line:
- To draw a downtrend line, connect the series of lower highs using a straight line. The line should be drawn above the price bars.

- Once at least two lower highs are connected, extending the line to the right can help identify potential resistance levels in the future.
   - Similar to an uptrend line, the more times the price touches or bounces off the downtrend line without breaking it, the more significant the trend line becomes.

4. Validating Trend Lines:
   - Trend lines are more reliable when they have been tested multiple times, with price bounces occurring at various points along the line.
   - However, there will be instances where a trend line is broken, indicating a potential trend reversal, and it's important to adapt and adjust accordingly.

5. Trend Line Breakouts:
   - A breakout occurs when the stock's price moves above an uptrend line or below a downtrend line.
   - Breakouts can signal a change in trend direction and may present trading opportunities, but confirmation through other analysis techniques is often advised.

By studying trend lines on stock charts, traders and investors can gain insights into the stock's price direction, identify potential support and resistance levels, and make more informed decisions when buying or selling options contracts. It's important to understand that trend lines are not foolproof predictors of future price movements.

Conclusion

"Don't watch the clock; do what it does. Keep going." - Sam Levenson

Overview

So, now you know that the world of stocks and options offers exciting opportunities for investors. The journey through this book has illuminated key concepts, strategies, and techniques that can help navigate this complex and dynamic market. From understanding the basics of stock valuation and market analysis to delving into the intricacies of options trading, readers have gained insights into the tools and knowledge necessary to make informed investment decisions. However, it is essential to recognize that investing in stocks and options carries inherent risks, and careful consideration must be given to individual risk tolerance, financial goals, and thorough research. By using this book as a foundation, readers can embark on their own investment journeys, armed with a solid understanding of stocks and options, and the confidence to navigate the ever-changing investment landscape.

Remember, successful investing requires continuous learning, adaptation, and a disciplined approach to achieve long-term financial success. Here's a brief recap on stocks and options:

1. Stocks: Stocks, or shares, represent ownership in a company. When you buy a stock, you become a shareholder and have a stake in the company's success. The value of stocks can fluctuate based on various factors such as company performance, market conditions, and investor sentiment. Investing in stocks can provide the potential for capital appreciation (the value of the stock increasing over time) and may also offer dividend payments, which are a portion of the company's profits distributed to shareholders.

2. Options: Options are financial derivatives that give the holder the right, but not the obligation, to buy or sell a specific underlying asset (such as a stock) at a predetermined price (strike price) within a specified period of time. There are two types of options: call options and put options. A call option gives the holder the right to buy the underlying asset, while a put option gives the holder the right to sell the underlying asset. Options allow investors to speculate on the price movement of the underlying asset or to hedge against potential losses.

Options can be used for various strategies, including:

- Buying calls to benefit from anticipated price increases.
- Buying puts to profit from expected price declines.
- Selling covered calls to generate income if you already own the underlying asset.
- Employing complex options spreads to limit risk or potentially profit from specific market scenarios.

It's important to note that options trading can be complex and involves risks, including the potential loss of the premium paid for the option. It generally requires a good understanding of market dynamics and thorough research.

Both stocks and options play significant roles in investment portfolios, with stocks providing long-term ownership and potential growth, while options offer opportunities for speculation or risk management. It's always recommended to research and understand the risks involved in any investment strategy before making any investment decisions. Additionally, seeking advice from a financial professional can provide valuable insights and guidance.

Benefits Of Investing In Stocks And Options

Here is a review of some of the benefits of investing in stocks and options:

Potential for Capital Appreciation:
Stocks have the potential to generate
significant returns over time. By investing in
well-performing companies, shareholders
can benefit from the appreciation of the
stock's value.

Dividend Income: Many companies
distribute a portion of their profits as
dividends to their shareholders. These
dividends can provide a regular stream of
income to investors, which can be
particularly valuable for income-focused
investors.

Ownership and Voting Rights: When
you buy stocks, you become a partial owner
of the company. This ownership can provide
voting rights and the ability to participate in
decision-making through proxy voting.

Portfolio Diversification: Investing in
stocks allows you to diversify your
investment portfolio. By spreading your
investments across different stocks and
sectors, you can potentially reduce risk and
enhance potential returns.

Liquidity: Stocks are generally highly
liquid investments, meaning they can be
easily bought or sold in the stock market.

This allows investors to quickly convert their investments into cash if needed.

Long-Term Growth: Historically, stocks have delivered higher long-term returns compared to other asset classes, such as bonds or cash. Investing in stocks can be an effective strategy to achieve wealth accumulation and financial goals over the long term.

Inflation Hedge: Investing in stocks can provide a hedge against inflation. Companies can potentially raise prices to adjust for inflation, which can lead to higher revenues and profits and consequently drive stock prices up.

Access to Professional Management: Investing in stocks also provides an opportunity to invest in mutual funds or exchange-traded funds (ETFs), which are managed by financial professionals. These investments offer diversification and expert management even for individual investors.

Remember, mistakes and setbacks are a natural part of the investment journey, but they also provide valuable learning experiences. Stay disciplined, stay curious, and never stop educating yourself about different investment opportunities and strategies.

I wish you all the best as you venture into the world
of financial investing. May your journey be filled
with valuable insights, rewarding experiences, and,
ultimately, financial freedom.

Glossary

These are just a few investment terms to help expand your knowledge. Remember to conduct further research and seek professional advice before making investment decisions.

Account holder: An individual or entity that holds an account with a financial institution, such as a bank or brokerage firm.

Adaptability: The ability to adjust and change according to new circumstances or conditions.

Asset: Anything that holds value and can be owned or controlled to generate future economic benefits.

At-the-Money (ATM): When the price of the underlying asset is nearly equal to the strike price of the option.

Bearish: A market sentiment indicating pessimism and an expectation of falling prices.

Bear Market: A period of declining stock prices and negative investor sentiment.

Blue-Chip Stocks: Stocks of large, well-established, and financially stable companies

Board members: Individuals elected or appointed to represent the interests of shareholders and provide oversight of a company's management, often playing a role in decision-making and corporate governance.with a history of reliable performance.

Breakout: A significant price movement that breaks through a key level of support or resistance, often accompanied by increased volume and signaling a potential change in the prevailing trend.

Bullish: A market sentiment indicating optimism and an expectation of rising prices.

Bull Market: A period of rising stock prices and positive investor sentiment.

Call Option: An option that gives the holder the right to buy the underlying asset at a predetermined price before the expiration date.

Candlestick Chart: A type of chart that displays price movements using candlestick-shaped symbols. Each candlestick represents a specific time period and shows the opening, closing, high, and low prices.

Capital: Generally refers to financial resources or wealth used for investment purposes. It can encompass funds contributed by investors, borrowed money, or retained earnings.

Capitalism: An economic system based on private ownership of the means of production and the pursuit of profit. In capitalism, individuals and businesses operate in a competitive market with limited government intervention.

Capital appreciation: The increase in the value of an asset or investment over time. It represents the potential gain from the rise in market prices.

Commodities: Raw materials or primary agricultural products that are traded in financial markets, such as gold, oil, wheat, or natural gas. Commodities are often used as inputs in the production of goods and services.

Compounding: The process of earning returns on an investment's initial principal as well as on any previously earned returns. Over time, compounding can significantly increase the value of an investment due to the reinvestment of earnings.

Consumer goods: Products that are purchased for personal use or consumption by individuals. Examples of consumer goods include food, clothing, electronics, household items, and automobiles.

Delta: Measures the rate of change in option price relative to changes in the underlying asset price.

Demand: The desire, willingness, and ability of consumers to purchase goods or services at a given price.

Derivatives: Financial contracts or instruments whose value is derived from an underlying asset, such as stocks, bonds, commodities, or indices. Examples of derivatives include options, futures contracts, and swaps.

Diversification: Spreading investments across different asset classes to reduce risk.

Dividend: A portion of a company's earnings distributed to its shareholders.

Dow Jones Industrial Average: A stock market index that tracks the performance of 30 large publicly traded companies in the United States, providing an indicator of the overall health of the U.S. stock market.

Dollar cost averaging: A strategy of investing a fixed amount of money at regular intervals regardless of market conditions. This approach allows investors to buy more shares when prices are lower and fewer shares when prices are higher, potentially reducing the overall average cost per share over time.

Downtrend: A prolonged period where the price of a security, market, or economic indicator experiences a consistent downward movement.

Earnings reports: Financial statements released by companies on a quarterly or annual basis, providing details about their revenues, expenses, profits, and losses. Earnings reports help investors evaluate a company's financial performance and make investment decisions.

Employment: The act of being engaged in paid work or having a job, typically referring to the number of people currently working or actively seeking employment.

ETF: An investment fund traded on stock exchanges, similar to a mutual fund but with shares that can be bought and sold throughout the trading day.

Executives: Individuals at the highest level of management within a company, responsible for making strategic decisions and overseeing the day-to-day operations.

Exchange Rate: The rate at which one currency can be exchanged for.

Expense Ratio: The annual fees charged by a mutual fund or ETF, expressed as a percentage of the fund's assets.

Expiration Date: The date on which an option contract expires, and the right to buy or sell the underlying asset is no longer valid.

Fibonacci Retracement: A tool used to identify potential levels of support or resistance based on the Fibonacci sequence, a series of numbers in which each number is the sum of the two preceding ones.

Financial advisor: A professional who provides guidance and advice on various financial matters, such as investments, retirement planning, tax strategies, and risk management.

Fixed income securities: Investments that provide a steady stream of income at regular intervals, such as government or corporate bonds.

Forex: Abbreviation for "foreign exchange," referring to the global market for trading currencies.

Fractional shares: Ownership of a fraction or portion of a single share of a stock or security. Fractional shares enable investors to own portions of expensive stocks or allocate smaller amounts of capital across multiple investments.

FTSE 100: An index that represents the 100 largest companies listed on the London Stock Exchange, often used as a gauge of the performance of the UK stock market.

Futures: Financial contracts that obligate buyers and sellers to trade an asset (commodity, currency, etc.) at a predetermined price and date in the future.

Gamma: Measures the rate of change in delta for a $1 change in the underlying asset price.

GDP growth: The percentage increase in the gross domestic product (GDP) of a country over a specific period, used to gauge economic growth.

Geopolitical: Relating to the influence of political and geopolitical events or factors on economic, financial, and investment landscapes. Geopolitical factors can include government policies, trade agreements, wars, or conflicts.

Greeks: Greek letters used to represent various measures of risk and sensitivity in options trading.

Implied Volatility: The market's expectation of how much a stock's price will fluctuate in the future, as implied by the option prices.

Index Fund: A mutual fund or ETF that aims to replicate the performance of a specific market index by holding the same securities in the same proportions as the index.

Individual Retirement Account (IRA): A tax-advantaged investment account that individuals can use to save and invest for retirement.

Industries: More specific groupings within sectors, representing companies involved in related or similar lines of business. For example, within the healthcare sector, industries can include pharmaceuticals, biotechnology, healthcare services, or medical devices.

Inflation rate: The rate at which the general level of prices for goods and services is increasing over time, eroding the purchasing power of money.

Inherently: In a natural or essential manner, implying that a particular characteristic or quality is an inherent or intrinsic part of something.

Initial Public Offering (IPO): The first sale of a company's stock to the public.

Interest: The cost of borrowing money or the return earned on an investment. It can refer to the interest charged on loans or the interest received on savings accounts or bonds.

Interest rate: The percentage charged or paid for the use of money, usually expressed as an annual percentage rate (APR).

In-the-Money (ITM): When the price of the underlying asset is favorable for the holder of the option to exercise and make a profit.

Intrinsic Value: The value of an option if it were to be exercised immediately, calculated as the difference between the current price of the underlying asset and the strike price.

Investor sentiment: The overall attitude or feelings of investors towards the market or a particular investment, which can influence their buying or selling decisions.

Limit Order: An order to buy or sell a security at a specific price (limit price) or better.

Liquidity: The ease with which an investment or asset can be bought or sold without causing significant price fluctuations.

MACD (Moving Average Convergence Divergence): A trend-following momentum indicator that shows the relationship between two moving averages of an asset's price. It consists of a MACD line, signal line, and histogram.

Market Capitalization: The total value of a company's outstanding shares of stock.

Market Order: A type of order to buy or sell a security at the best available current market price.

Mitigate: To reduce or minimize the severity, impact, or risk of something. In investing, mitigating risk could involve taking steps to minimize potential losses or protect against adverse events.

Moving Average (MA): A technical indicator that calculates the average price over a specified period. It helps smooth out price fluctuations and identify trends.

Mutual Fund: An investment vehicle that pools money from multiple investors to invest in a diversified portfolio of securities managed by professional portfolio managers.

NASDAQ: An electronic stock exchange in the United States where many technology and growth companies are listed, known for its high-tech and speculative stocks.

Net Asset Value (NAV): The per-share value of a mutual fund, calculated by dividing the total value of the fund's assets by the number of shares.

Optimism: A positive or hopeful outlook, often associated with an expectation for favorable outcomes or market conditions.

Option Premium: The price paid to purchase an option contract.

Option Spread: A strategy involving the simultaneous purchase and sale of different options with different strike prices or expiration dates.

Option: A financial derivative contract that gives the buyer the right (not the obligation) to buy (call option) or sell (put option) a specific asset (e.g., stock) at a predetermined price within a specific time frame.

Oscillator: A technical indicator that fluctuates between defined levels or bands to indicate overbought or oversold conditions, helping traders identify potential reversals.

Out of the Money (OTM): An option with no intrinsic value because the stock price is not favorable compared to the strike price (for call options, the stock price is below the strike price, and for put options, the stock price is above the strike price).

Penny Stocks: Stocks with low prices, typically traded outside major stock exchanges, and considered to be highly speculative.

Portfolio: A collection of investments held by an investor.

Predetermined: Decided or established in advance, often referring to a fixed plan or course of action.

Premium: The price paid by the option buyer to the option seller for the rights associated with the contract.

Profitability: The ability of a business or investment to generate profit or positive financial returns. It is a measure of how effectively an entity utilizes its resources to generate earnings.

Prudent: Acting with caution, sound judgment, and careful consideration, typically in relation to financial or investment decisions.

Pump and dump schemes: Illegal activities whereby individuals or groups artificially inflate the price of a particular investment, typically through deceptive or misleading information, and then sell off their holdings for a profit once the price has risen.

Put Option: A type of option that gives the holder the right, but not the obligation, to sell the underlying asset at a predetermined price (strike price) within a specified timeframe.

Real estate: Property consisting of land, buildings, and natural resources. Real estate can be used for various purposes, including residential, commercial, industrial, or agricultural.

Real estate investment trusts (REITs): Companies that own, operate, or finance income-generating real estate properties. REITs allow investors to gain exposure to real estate assets without directly owning or managing them.

Recession: A significant decline in economic activity characterized by a contraction in GDP, lower employment rates, reduced consumer spending, and decreased business output.

Resilience: The ability to withstand and recover from adversity or market fluctuations, often used to describe the strength and endurance of an investment or portfolio.

Resistance: A price level at which sellers typically emerge, preventing further upward movement, creating a ceiling for the asset's price.

Return: The gain or loss on an investment, usually expressed as a percentage.

Rho: Measures the sensitivity of option price to changes in interest rates.

Risk-Return Tradeoff: The principle that higher returns typically involve taking on greater levels of investment risk.

Risk Tolerance: An individual's ability to withstand fluctuations in the value of investments without panicking or making irrational decisions.

Robo-advisors: Online platforms or digital tools that provide automated investment advice and portfolio management services, typically using algorithms and computer algorithms.

Roth IRA/401(k): Retirement accounts with after-tax contributions, but qualified withdrawals are tax-free.

RSI (Relative Strength Index): A momentum oscillator that measures the speed and change of price movements. RSI moves between 0 and 100, with levels above 70 indicating overbought conditions and levels below 30 indicating oversold conditions.

Securities: Stocks, Options, and bonds

S&P 500: Abbreviation for the Standard & Poor's 500, an index that measures the performance of 500 large companies listed on U.S. stock exchanges, widely used as a benchmark for the overall U.S. stock market.

Sectors: Broad categories that classify companies based on the nature of their business activities. Common sectors include technology, healthcare, consumer goods, financials, and energy, among others.

Spread: A strategy involving the simultaneous buying and selling of options on the same underlying asset, with different strike prices or expiration dates.

Standardized: Made consistent or uniform by establishing standards or guidelines, ensuring a common measure or benchmark.

Stock: A share of ownership in a company.

Stock Market or Stock Exchange: A physical or virtual marketplace where stocks are bought and sold.

Stop loss orders: An order placed by an investor to sell a security automatically if it reaches a specific price, known as the stop price. Stop loss orders are used to limit losses or protect gains by triggering an automatic sale at a predetermined price level.

Strike Price: The predetermined price at which the underlying asset can be bought or sold through an option contract.

Support: A price level at which buyers are expected to enter and prevent further downward movement, creating a floor for the asset's price.

Tax deductible: Expenses or items that can be deducted from income when calculating taxable income, resulting in a reduction of the overall tax liability.

Terms and conditions: The rules, requirements, and provisions that govern a contract or agreement, outlining the rights and obligations of the parties involved.

Theta: Measures the rate of decline in option value as time passes, also known as time decay.

Traditional IRA/401(k): Retirement accounts with pre-tax contributions, and taxes are paid upon withdrawal.

Transactions: Financial activities involving the buying, selling, or exchange of goods, services, or financial instruments.

Trend: The direction in which a market or asset is moving, either upwards (bullish), downwards (bearish), or sideways (range-bound).

Trend reversal: A point at which the direction of a trend changes, transitioning from a downtrend to an uptrend, or vice versa.

Uptrend: A prolonged period where the price of a security, market, or economic indicator experiences a consistent upward movement.

Value: The worth or monetary estimation of an asset or investment, often determined by factors such as its earning potential, cash flow, and market conditions.

Volatility: A measure of the price swings or fluctuations of a stock. High volatility implies greater uncertainty.

Volume: The number of shares, contracts, or units traded during a given period. Volume can provide insights into the strength of price movements or indicate potential trend reversals.

References

At the money definition. IG. (n.d.).
https://www.ig.com/en/glossary-trading-terms/at-the-money-definition#:~:text=At%20the%20money%20(ATM)%20is,so%20close%20to%20becoming%20profitable.

Chen, J. (n.d.). *Extrinsic value: Definition, how to calculate, and example.* Investopedia.
https://www.investopedia.com/terms/e/extrinsicvalue.asp

Chen, J. (n.d.-a). Stock analysis: Different methods for evaluating stocks. Investopedia.
https://www.investopedia.com/terms/s/stock-analysis.asp

Chen, J. (n.d.-b). Technical indicator: Definition, analyst uses, types and examples. Investopedia.
https://www.investopedia.com/terms/t/technicalindicator.asp

Chen, J. (n.d.-c). Trendline: What it is, how to use it in investing, with examples. Investopedia.
https://www.investopedia.com/terms/t/trendline.asp

Chen, J. (n.d.-d). What are options? types, spreads, example, and risk metrics. Investopedia. https://www.investopedia.com/terms/o/option.asp

Chen, J. (n.d.-e). What is a brokerage account? definition, how to choose, and types. Investopedia. https://www.investopedia.com/terms/b/brokerage account.asp

Dictionary.com. (n.d.). Dictionary.com. https://www.dictionary.com/

Dierking, D. (n.d.). Benefits of holding stocks for the long-term. Investopedia. https://www.investopedia.com/articles/investing/052216/4-benefits-holding-stocks-long-term.asp

Downey, L. (n.d.). 10 options strategies every investor should know. Investopedia. https://www.investopedia.com/trading/options-str ategies/

Editors, T. T. (n.d.). Credit vs. debit spreads: Let volatility guide you. https://tickertape.tdameritrade.com/amp/trading/option-credit-spreads-option-debit-spreads-17838

Farley, A. (n.d.-a). Simple and effective exit trading strategies. Investopedia. https://www.investopedia.com/articles/active-trad ing/020915/mustknow-simple-effective-exit-tradin g-strategies.asp

Farley, A. (n.d.-b). What is a candlestick pattern?. Investopedia. https://www.investopedia.com/articles/active-trad ing/092315/5-most-powerful-candlestick-patterns. asp

Girardin, M., & Girardin   →, M. (2023, March 17). What is an asset? definition and examples. Forage. https://www.theforage.com/blog/skills/asset#:~:te xt=An%20asset%20is%20generally%20any,can%2 0also%20be%20an%20asset.

Hayes, A. (n.d.-a). Dividends: Definition in stocks and how payments work. Investopedia. https://www.investopedia.com/terms/d/dividend. asp

Hayes, A. (n.d.-b). Technical analysis: What it is and how to use it in investing. Investopedia. https://www.investopedia.com/terms/t/technicala nalysis.asp#:~:text=Key%20Takeaways-,Technical %20analysis%20is%20a%20trading%20discipline %20employed%20to%20evaluate%20investments,t he%20security's%20future%20price%20movement s.

Hayes, A. (n.d.-c). What are greeks in finance and how are they used?. Investopedia. https://www.investopedia.com/terms/g/greeks.asp

Mitchell, C. (n.d.-a). Breakout: Definition, meaning, example, and what it tells you. Investopedia. https://www.investopedia.com/terms/b/breakout. asp#:~:text=A%20breakout%20is%20when%20the ,Breakouts%20provide%20possible%20trading%20 opportunities.

Mitchell, C. (n.d.). *How to use stock volume to improve your trading*. Investopedia. https://www.investopedia.com/articles/technical/ 02/010702.asp

Mitchell, C. (n.d.-b). Only take a trade if it passes this 5-step test. Investopedia. https://www.investopedia.com/articles/active-trad ing/090415/only-take-trade-if-it-passes-5step-test. asp

Mitchell, C. (n.d.-c). Understanding basic candlestick charts. Investopedia. https://www.investopedia.com/trading/candlestick -charting-what-is-it/

Schwab.com. (n.d.). 5 steps for choosing stocks. Schwab Brokerage. https://international.schwab.com/content/5-steps- choosing-stocks

Segal, T. (n.d.). Fundamental analysis: Principles, types, and how to use it. Investopedia. https://www.investopedia.com/terms/f/fundament alanalysis.asp

Shockdav, & Tsadmin. (2020, January 7). 10 tips to manage your emotions while trading. TraderSync. https://tradersync.com/10-tips-to-manage-your-emotions-while-trading/

Smith, L. (2022, October 28). On the spot: How to enter and Exit A Forex Trade. iExpats. https://www.iexpats.com/on-the-spot-how-to-enter-and-exit-a-forex-trade/#:~:text=Every%20trader%20should%20have%20a,movement%20eating%20into%20your%20gains.

Summa, J. (n.d.). Option greeks: The 4 factors to measure risk. Investopedia. https://www.investopedia.com/trading/getting-to-know-the-greeks/

Weltman, B. (n.d.). How stock options are taxed and reported. Investopedia. https://www.investopedia.com/articles/active-trading/061615/how-stock-options-are-taxed-reported.asp

What is portfolio diversification?. Fidelity. (n.d.). https://www.fidelity.com/learning-center/investment-products/mutual-funds/diversification#:~:text=Diversification%20is%20the%20practice%20of,of%20your%20portfolio%20over%20time.